INSIDERS GUIDE TO CAMPGROUND HOSTING IN FLORIDA PARKS

FREE CAMPSITES FOR VOLUNTEERING

Jolene MacFadden

Full-Time RVer, Volunteer and Writer

Copyright 2014 by Jolene MacFadden

All Rights Reserved

ISBN-13: 978-1502599957

ISBN-10: 1502599953

ACKNOWLEDGEMENTS

We would like to thank all the Florida State Parks, Florida State Forests, Florida County Parks and Recreation Departments, Florida Water Management Districts, Florida Wildlife Management Areas, Florida National Parks and Forests Volunteer Coordinators and Managers who answered my emails and took my phone calls to make this book a reality. Without their assistance it would not have been possible to finish it in a timely manner.

I would also like to thank my mom and younger daughter for their patience while I was sequestered away trying to collect the information and write the book. They helped get our volunteer duties done and allowed me the space to compile the information needed. And to my other children and family who always encourages me to keep trying new things. Thanks so much!

THIS PAGE LEFT BLANK

Table of Contents

INTRODUCTION 3
INFORMATION FOR NEWBIES 5
    Be Prepared for Emergencies 5
    A Couple of Thoughts on Park Amenities for Live On-Site Volunteers .. 5
    Skills Required Of Campground/Park/Residential Hosts 7
    DISCLAIMER 9
FLORIDA STATE PARKS 10
    The Beginning Process 11
    References and Background Checks 12
    A Word on Communications 12
    The Benefits 14
    The Downsides 16
    The Jobs 19
    New Live On-Site Volunteers Considerations 45
    Things to Consider Before Applying at any Florida Park 46
    Volunteer Timesheet Info 47
    Florida State Parks with Live On-Site Volunteers 48
    Florida State Parks - Plans for Future Campground/Residential/Parks Hosts Sites 149
FLORIDA COUNTY PARKS 152
FLORIDA STATE FORESTS 187
OTHER STATE AGENCIES IN FLORIDA WITH CAMPGROUND/PARK HOST POSITIONS 196
    Florida Fish and Wildlife 196
    Florida Water Management Districts 199
NATIONAL AGENCIES 207
    National Forests 208
    National Parks 219
    U.S. Army Corp of Engineers 239
    U.S. Fish and Wildlife 241
END OF BOOK CREDITS AND AUTHOR INFORMATION 258

About The Author 259
Connect With Me 260

INTRODUCTION

My mom and I have been traveling around the state of Florida for the last 2 years visiting our state parks and decided to become campground hosts to help pay some of tour expenses. Yes, you can get a job being a campground host at the ritzy RV parks around the state and some will even pay you a little something to go along with having a place to park your RV or travel trailer with water, electric, sewer, etc., but there is nothing like the great outdoors, being in a tranquil setting and giving your time and experience to those who appreciate it the most.

Our Florida State, County and National Parks and Forests, like most around the country, are in desperate need of people willing to donate their time, energy and experience to keep them maintained, cleaned and available for all visitors. These parks are a great educational tool for our younger generations as well as a place to enjoy the great outdoors with your family and friends. We have gathered as much information as we can about the Florida State Parks, Florida National Parks and Forests, Florida County Parks and Wildlife and Water Management Areas to give you more opportunities to explore Florida, learn new skills and help where help is needed.

In the following pages we have included the important information about these places that offer FREE campsites for volunteers. We list the parks, who to contact, what amenities they offer, some of the duties they require, the hours they require of "live on-side volunteers" and the times they really need the most help.

We hope you will consider volunteering in our great public Florida Recreational Areas. They could use your help and most of the personnel really appreciate your time and efforts spent on their behalf. And we know their visitors do.

This type of volunteering is not just for those who have retired and are wondering around the country in a tricked-out RV Rig. It can be for those who just want to spend a couple of months in the great outdoors but cannot afford to pay to stay at a RV resort. If you have any kind of travel trailer or RV (in some cases a tent or even a boat with sleeping quarters), are able to pay for your own food and gas and any of your other monthly expenses then you can be a volunteer campground and/or park host in one of our great Florida Parks. This would be great for writers, teachers, college students or anyone taking a few months off from work and just needs a place to park their camper, work a few hours a day and have the rest of the time to relax, write a book, explore the trails, learn about ecology and history, work on your online business, or just hang out with your fellow campers. The summer time is the hardest time to get volunteers here in Florida. So that makes it a great time for you to begin your volunteer career!

We truly believe that volunteering in one of our many state, county and national parks, forest and management areas will benefit you as well and the parks' themselves. You will gather memories, take pictures, make new friends and have great adventures to tell your family and friends about for years to come. We hope you will find the information in this guide useful and that you will decide to take a chance and join the rest of us here in one of the many great Florida Parks!

INFORMATION FOR NEWBIES

Be Prepared for Emergencies

When traveling, volunteering and even at home, you should be prepared for bad weather. In Florida, especially during hurricane season, you want to be prepared to evacuate. When you volunteer at a State, County or National Park or Forest you will be asked to leave the parks when threatening weather is coming. The park personnel are legally obligated to evacuate all visitors and personnel. Another example is when the Federal Government shut down last year and everyone in the National Parks had to leave because they had no "budget".

It is always a good idea to have a plan in place, just in case. I know we are not very good about this either but it should be noted that you might want to make sure your RV and personal vehicles have full tanks of gas and propane at all times. We recommend personal possessions replacement insurance should the worse happen to go along with your vehicle and camper rig insurance policies. You really should have an emergency cash reserve stashed away so that you can have ready access to it.

And, when you arrive at your new volunteer assignment check with the Volunteer Coordinator for where the nearest emergency shelters are located should an evacuation order be given. They should have this information handy. That way when the crisis has passed you can return to help the park staff with the clean-up. A lot of volunteers just walked away from their assignments when this happens. I know it is hard to come back to a place you were asked to leave but they will need the volunteers even more once the crisis has passed. Of course, if you feel you have to leave the area we hope you will tell the Volunteer Coordinator your plans so that they will not be expecting you back again.

A Couple of Thoughts on Park Amenities for Live On-Site Volunteers

When reviewing what the parks offer their potential live on-site volunteers you need to make sure of a couple of things before your final decision.

RV/Trailer Rig Length Limits: You will need to ask if their live on-site campsites set aside for the volunteers is long enough to accommodate your rig. We have a 31 foot Class "A" Rig so we could never stay at Little Talbot Island State Park as their limit is 30 feet. The volunteer coordinator at the park will ask you the length of you rig before you come so that they will make sure the site they assign to you will fit. On the other hand, we got our assignment at Myakka River State Park, in part, because our rig was only 31 foot. The couple who use to have the assignment got a new, longer rig and they couldn't be assigned to the Old Prairie Campground.

Campsite Amenities: Water/Electric/Sewer – Not all the Florida Parks offer sewers on their campground sites and some don't even have them on the sites in their "Volunteer Village" area either. This is pretty important to me and my mom as we do have a Class "A" rig and have to drive to the Dump Station every two days to dump our Gray and Black Water Tanks. We do not have a "Blue Boy" nor do we have the capacity to tow one. If you own one and don't mind using them then more power to you!

We did that at St. Josephs Peninsula State Park during the entire two months we were there and it was a real drag. It made my brother happy though as we had to start the motor every two or three days and drive around to the dump station and back.

Electrical Types: Not all of the state parks have 50Amp Electrical Outlets. Most of the newer, bigger types of campers require 50Amp service to run all their equipment. If you have one of these you might have to compromise with a step-down attachment and then not be able to use all of your appliances. The parks are slowly replacing the older boxes with newer ones in order to accommodate these newer units. This is a very slow process and has to be planned in advanced so that the park can get the funding in the budget.

Our Rig only has 30Amps and we are able to run our A/C and our other appliances just fine. We only can run one A/C unit at a time and we do not have a Washer/Dryer unit or any other big electrical appliances.

FREE Extras: One of the Free Extras we really look for is the use of a washer/dryer. Not all the parks have laundry facilities for their volunteers let alone their regular campers. This can be a problem as it costs quite a bit of money these days to find a Laundromat and pay to have your clothes cleaned. This can cut into your budget as well as the time and expense of going out of the park each week. Living in this small space full-time doesn't leave a lot of room for clothes. We only have about a week's worth of clothes for each of us so we have to do laundry as often as possible.

We don't really do campfires, so Free Firewood, has never been a consideration. But if you are one of those people that enjoy a good campfire you will probably look for this extra. Paying for firewood will also cut into your monthly budget.

Another thing that some of the parks might offer is free ice. Most have their own ice machines and volunteers can get just about as much as they need. The only time this has really been important to us is during the hot summer months or when we have people visiting us. It is just one more expense when we have to pay for it. But if the park offers it for free then it is a nice extra.

Skills Required Of Campground/Park/Residential Hosts

A lot of newbies will ask themselves if they have the skills required to be a campground host, park host and/or residential host in any of the Florida State Parks. My mom and I both worked mainly in office jobs. I mean we raised our kids, cooked, cleaned, etc. So we do have some natural skills required as most of what the parks need is for people to help clean bathrooms, park buildings, pick up trash and empty trash cans. They also need people who are friendly to guests when greeting them, answering any questions they may have and direct them to park facilities. Sometimes you will have to mow some grass, use a blower to blow off the roads and sidewalks and trim some branches. We have all done a little yard work in our lifetimes. If not the park rangers will be happy to show you how to use the equipment.

My favorite is the 360-Riding Lawn Mower. It turns completely around "on a dime". It only took about 5 minutes for the ranger to show me how to work it and another hour or so to practice mowing up and down a clear area of lawn before I felt comfortable enough to jump on and mow anytime it was needed to be done. The gas blower was the same. The hardest part is to get those things started because most of them are old and don't want to start cold.

For Those Handy-Persons or mechanically inclined: If you have carpentry, plumbing, electrical or mechanic skills as a professional or hobby then you can pretty much get a volunteer assignment at just about any of the Florida Park or Management Area. The budgets for our state parks, forests and management areas are so restricted that there just isn't any money for new equipment that is so badly needed. The parks have to make do with what they have or donations from their Friends Groups. Keeping all the old equipment, vehicles, and buildings in use is a constant battle for most of the parks. So a good handyperson is always needed.

If you are thinking of doing the Full Time RVing thing and volunteering in any state, federal or local parks to help with expenses then we would suggest that you take some beginners mechanic courses, electrical, plumbing and/or carpentry classes at your local community school. These skills are highly sought after all over the country.

For the most part, all the Florida Parks, Forests and Management Areas are looking for people willing to learn new things, be customer-service oriented, and work hard getting the assigned tasks done as quickly and thoroughly as possible.

Remember once you have completed your assignments for the day you don't have to drive anywhere to enjoy your off time in some of the most beautiful areas because you are already there!

DISCLAIMER

All the information given here is as accurate as we can make it at the time we have published this book. Just remember people change jobs all the time, volunteer opportunities may be already booked for the time you want, new duties may be added or changed, and the hours required may change, and sometimes the park may add or take away amenities for the volunteer sites and positions. As with anything in life you will need to verify it for yourself by contacting the parks you would like to spend some time volunteering in directly. Ask lots of questions and if you can visit the park as a guest before volunteering, even better. If not, you can always look online and read reviews from your fellow campers, watch videos on YouTube and ask questions in the Workamper forums and group pages on websites and social media sites.

Yes, some of this information is already on our website and available for free but most of it is not. We have tried to create a comprehensive resource with this book so that anyone who is willing to commit their time, energy and expertise when volunteering will have the most pertinent information available to schedule volunteer assignments all year long. Our various national, state and county parks depend on volunteers and we want you to know what you are getting into before you look for these assignments.

FLORIDA STATE PARKS

There are about 170 Florida State Parks and Trails which is governed by the Florida Department of Environmental Protection. Volunteers are a big part of the park system and they supplement the park staff to help keep our parks going. Not only do they have local, day volunteers but about 100 state parks have "live on-site" volunteers. These positions include campground hosts, residential hosts, maintenance hosts and/or park hosts that do a variety of different jobs for that state park. These parks offer FREE campsites in exchange for 20 to 40 hours per week per campsite. Some of you may say 20 to 40 hours per week is too much for someone who is just looking to work a little in exchange for free utilities and a place to park their recreational vehicle. You may be right about that but you might also consider the following factors before deciding:

Will I be getting some added benefits such as free laundry facilities, free ice, and free wood, discounted fees on canoe rentals, etc. that will help defray some of my costs?

Is it the type of park I would like to spend more time in to explore, use the facilities and take advantage of the many services they offer?

And these questions you may not be able to answer until after you have been there for a little while:

Are my services really appreciated by the staff and visitors?

Are my services really needed to help the staff keep the park clean, maintained and repaired or am I working just so the staff can goof off elsewhere?

There are probably many more questions you can ask yourself before you accept any kind of assignment like volunteering in a Florida State Park as a campground host, residential host or park host.

The most important things to consider before you accept any assignment are:

What are the hours they are asking of me?

Am I able to do the duties they require?

Do I believe that what they offer in exchange for my time is worth it to me?

The Beginning Process

Everything has a beginning, middle and end and so does becoming a campground host/park host in Florida State Parks. For most people you will fill out an application online, decide which parks or regions you would like to serve and wait for a response from the parks. With a little bit of research and patience you might be able to hurry that aspect of the application process along.

Let's face it, all the state parks located on the Atlantic Ocean and Gulf of Mexico really do not have all that much trouble getting help all through the year. We got a summer assignment for 2 months at TH Stone Memorial St. Joseph's Peninsula State Park on the Gulf of Mexico because their regular couples could not come. Granted, being on the ocean during the start of hurricane season was not our first choice and that park does not offer sewers on-site for campground hosts but we wanted to try it anyway. It was hard work and we got out before the really bad weather started up. We had a pretty good time none-the-less.

Later in this book we will have a complete listing of all the Florida State Parks that are setup with campsites for volunteers that will help you narrow the focus of your application. And if you get some experience during the late spring and summer months in a few of the parks possibly some of the other parks along the coasts will start asking you to volunteer with them. Again, some of the process involves a little bit of luck and timing. We were offered a winter assignment in Southwest Florida because we were recommended by one of the park rangers vacationing in one of the other parks we were working at. You just never know who you are going to meet in these parks and if you are doing a good job, are customer-oriented, you just might start getting some really interesting assignments.

Everyone has to fill out an application. If you fill it out online it will be automatically sent to the District Volunteer Coordinator assigned to your choices listed on the application. Some people say it is better to put your top three parks on the application and others suggest that newbies just put the regions that interest them most. Of course, getting a call back depends on what months you are available and whether those parks need help during those times. You can always contact the parks directly to see if they have an opening for those time periods before you fill out the form.

Personally, I downloaded the application and filled it out to have on hand when we go searching for new assignments. When I need to apply for a new position I just copy and paste the information in the appropriate boxes. This is also handy if one of the parks asked for a signed copy of the application for their files. We have it ready and scanned in as an Acrobat Reader File along with a scanned copy of our Drivers Licenses. Some parks require that you have a valid Driver's License to drive the park's vehicles. They will also need to do a background check on all the applicants prior to accepting them as volunteers. It may take some time to hear back from the parks after you submit the online application. Be patient!

Go to the link below to get more information directly from the Florida State Parks website about applying, fill out the online application, download the application as well as the Volunteers Handbook. You will want to read through that booklet to familiarize yourself with some of the rules and regulations, benefits, etc. of being any type of volunteer with the state parks. This is a guide. Some of the parks may add their own forms, rules, and other things that pertain to their particular situation.

http://www.floridastateparks.org/getinvolved/volunteer.cfm

Download the Florida State Park Application to Fill Out and email to the state parks of your choice.

http://www.floridastateparks.org/Getinvolved/doc/volunteerapplication.pdf

References and Background Checks

Florida State Parks do conduct background checks and contact references. Most newbies will need to list former employers and friends as references. But those who have volunteered in other places should list the contact information for the Manager and/or Volunteer Coordinator instead. These types of references are great for showing you as a reliable and hard-working volunteer.

For those with a criminal record you will need to be honest on your application. They will be considered only on a case-by-case basis. Although some offenses automatically disqualify you as a volunteer others may not.

A Word on Communications

Sometimes we have called the parks we wanted to stay at directly before putting in an updated application. It is best to try to speak to the park's volunteer coordinator during regular business hours (Monday through Friday, 8:00am to 4:00pm) with mornings being better than afternoons. Please remember that park personnel are often called upon to do a variety of different jobs within the park and may not be able to talk to you right away. Nor will they be able to answer emails right away either. Generally, only the park's volunteer coordinator will be able to answer your questions. So be patient but persistent as well as polite to those who are trying to help you. It may take a couple of days for them to return phone calls and emails. It doesn't hurt to leave a message for them as well as sending an email with your questions. That way the coordinator will have the answers ready for you when they return your call.

On the other hand, if the volunteer coordinator has offered you a position they really need to hear back from you as quickly as possible. Sometimes, we also get busy and forget to return emails or phone messages. If you are trying to get a volunteer assignment it is best to handle those communications as businesslike as possible. It shows you have good communication skills and goes more towards proving that you are a reliable person.

If you don't want the assignment being offered then getting back to the coordinator is just as important. There is nothing wrong with asking for 24 hours to decide if you can take any potential assignment. Making sure you can do the job, are comfortable with the hours required and are able to be there to start when they need you and stay as long as they require. You should have already researched the park before applying for any of the positions and know that you would like to spend time there. But like I said being a good communicator is a great habit to have and is greatly appreciated.

The Benefits

There are a number of benefits to becoming a volunteer in our Florida State Parks. Not the least of which is a FREE campsite if you are campground host, park host or residential host. You will also get a very good sense of accomplishment when you do your jobs well; meet new and interesting people from all over the world, work with some really great, dedicated staff members and you will have helped keep our public resources going. Maintaining our parks, restoring historic places, and helping our park rangers with their programs to educate the public are all great services that not only benefit the general public but you, your friends and your family now and for future generations.

But you want to know what you will receive in exchange for your services:

**After 100 hours of service you should receive a pass to come back to that park anytime over the next 12 months.

The Volunteer handbook says you should receive a Volunteer ID after 100 hours but we have yet to receive one of those at any of the parks we have volunteered for. These are mostly for local volunteers who only volunteer at one park all year long.

**The Volunteer Hours Tabs for your Volunteer Name Tag have to be applied for as you achieve them by the Volunteer Coordinator/Manager of the park you are currently volunteering with. You can get them at 100, 250, 500 hours, 1000 hours and every 1000 after that. You will need to purchase your own metal Name Tag to hang these on though.

**After 500 hours of service you can fill out the request for the State of Florida Parks Pass. Now this we did get. It is good for 12 months from your application date and allows you FREE ENTRANCE into all the state Parks for you and up to 8 people in the car with you. *(Except the Skyway Fishing Pier or only 2 people to Weeki Wachee Springs State Park and Ellie Schiller Homosassa Springs Wildlife State Park)*

This we have applied for and gotten within 30 days. We were at Dade Battlefield Historic State Park at the time and the Manager was more than happy to sign the form and the Volunteer Coordinator verified the hours from our other parks then sent them into Tallahassee for us.

**Each park you volunteer for will give you a light gray volunteer T-Shirt; a black volunteer hat, if you need or want one and a blank State of Florida Parks name tag. At Myakka River State Park we got a gold toned magnetic name tag to wear while we were there. When we finished our assignment they asked for those back because they are a little expensive. The plastic black and gray name tags are pin backs and easily replaced.

**Every Florida State Park Volunteer is covered by Workers Compensation should they get hurt while performing their duties.

**Campground Hosts, Park Hosts, Residential Hosts and Maintenance Hosts who stay in the park for 2 to 4 months will get the use of a FREE Campsite that includes electric and water. Most are level sites and quite a few will have sewers on-site but not all. So if this is a priority for you make sure you ask before accepting any assignment. In the Parks section of this book we are trying to list all those basic amenities as we get the details from the parks. Some parks have free laundry facilities for the volunteers, free ice, free firewood and even the use of a golf cart.

**Of course, you get the run of the park while you are there and can use any of the facilities for you and your invited guests so long as they are not reserved for someone else. Sometimes you will have access to the tools and machines in the shop area should you need to fix something on your car or RV/Travel Trailer. Always ask before you borrow any of the park's equipment.

**We have even been offered the use of a furnished apartment for $20 a night at Myakka River State Park should some of our friends and family wanted to visit us during our stay. During the holidays the parks may even have parties for staff and volunteers as well as yearly volunteer and/or employee picnics. These get-togethers are always a nice benefit and give the volunteers the opportunity to meet each other and the other park personnel in a more informal and relaxed setting.

**Some parks with a gift shop will offer discounts on the merchandise for volunteers. You might even get discounted rates on canoes and kayaks that the park owns for your personal use. You just never know what benefits you will get in any of the parks that you are going to work for until you get there!

Just a sidebar note: Just because you are volunteering in the park doesn't mean you are "entitled" to get the run of the park, priority use of the facilities or able to borrow any of the equipment or tools. It is always better to ask permission before you use any of the park's resources. More than likely, if the Park Staff do not need the equipment or tools, or paying customers are not using the facilities you will be able to use them.

The Downsides

As with any work situation there are bound to be downsides to them. Some people may not consider these to be downsides and others may even think they may be deal breakers. But here are a few of the things we consider might be a downside to volunteering in any of our Florida Parks.

The bugs, the snakes, and the spiders.

You cannot do much of anything outdoors and not run into our insects, reptiles and arachnids. If you have a fear of these you might want to consider another alternative. But this is the state of Florida and you are going to be in the woods. So buy lots of insect repellent, snake-away and watch where you walk.

Working in sweltering heat during the summer months.

There is not a lot you can do about the weather. It is just something you will have to prepare for, take lots of breaks and drink lots of liquids. My mom and I usually keep a wet wash cloth in a plastic bag with us. You can splash some water on it, ring it out and place it on your neck, top of your head or even your wrists for a quick cool-down.

You actually have to work to get your FREE Campsite.

Yes, you really do have to do what is asked of you in exchange for all the great benefits you do receive. You are there to help the park staff get their projects done, keep the park clean and safe to use for all visitors.

Too many people visit these parks.

Depending on the park you accept an assignment with you will more than likely have to deal with the public. There are a few parks with limited public exposure but the whole point of volunteering as a Campground Host is to actually meet fellow campers, exchange stories, educate them about the park and encourage them to come back often with their friends and family.

If you have a particular skill such as carpentry, electrical or mechanical you will more than likely be able to help in their shop area keeping their equipment going, building new picnic tables and repairing their machines and buildings. These types of positions have very little public interaction. And some parks are small and/or out of the way that they do not receive a whole lot of visitors. If these are more to your liking then when you contact the park you want to volunteer in then ask how many visitors that they get during their average months. Here on the Suwannee River in the Suwannee River Wilderness Trail river camps we usually only get a couple of visitors at a time, some days none at all and a few time we get large groups that stay overnight then move on the next day.

I hate politics.

Yes, most of us hate the politics inherent in any work situation. I am sorry to say there really isn't much you can do about them except to work with them, around them or just don't come back to that park in the future. Some parks personnel and situations are worse than others. You will only learn about them through experience. You can always check the RV forums and group pages online for those campground hosts who have already volunteered at the parks you are visiting.

Please, remember that situations change when personnel change and even during different times of the year. Problems that occur during the "peak" season may not be present during the "off" season. And what was true last year may not be true this year.

They ask too much for what we are given.

Most of the park staff try their very best to keep your hours to the requested amount. If they ask for 20 hours then work 20 hours. If they asked for at least 24 then just work that amount. If you don't get everything done you can always finish it the next day. But if you want to finish or do more then go ahead and get it done.

Most rangers will try to work with you by allowing you an extra day off if you have put in too much time that week. Remember you are volunteering to help that park and the park staff accomplish their goals, educate the public and keep our resources available for our children and grandchildren. And, as always, every hour you volunteer in the park will make it better.

They didn't tell me I had to do that!

If you don't feel comfortable doing something new we hope you will express your feelings to the park ranger. He or She will do their best to make sure you are trained to do any job they ask of you. Remember, you are there to help them get their jobs done. Just try it the first time and if you really cannot do that particular job then be honest with them. There are so many things that needs to done in our parks there is bound to be some things you can do that would help out the staff and that you might enjoy more.

My agreed upon time is just too long.

If you agreed to work for that park for 4 months then you really should try to stick it out. Again, you will need to be honest with the volunteer coordinator when you accept any assignment and keep your commitments. Most parks want at least a 3 month commitment and some will allow 2 months. It really depends on their needs.

We suggest that newbies try to get a 2 month assignment first to see if being a campground host is something they really want to do. Hillsborough River State Park has even suggested that they will take on a new person, during the summer, for an initial 2 weeks and then if everyone is happy they will give you the option of an additional 2 months. Research your park choices and visit them before you commit if you can! But most of all, please, **BE HONEST** with the Volunteer Coordinator. Of course, emergencies can and do arise so if you have to leave your assignment early make sure you contact the park's volunteer coordinator as soon as possible.

I have to do paperwork, ugh!

Yes, with any bureaucracy there is bound to be lots of paperwork. Thankfully, as volunteers we only have to do a little bit of it when asked. Some of the parks we have volunteered for asked us to keep track of visitors and report the count every month. Other parks just wanted us to keep track of our supplies and do our timesheets. It really depends on what you are doing and where you are doing it. The paperwork is important though and may even help that park get more funding, personnel and equipment. Make sure you understand how to fill it out and when it is due. This is especially true of your timesheets. You want to get credit for the hours you have worked.

Why Do I Have to Attend Those Seminars?

We were very surprised we were required to read through the Sexual Harassment Awareness, Diversity Training and Code of Ethics Handbook every year just like the park staff. Because we are considered workers, non-paid though we are, and covered under their workers compensation and OSHA requirements we have to read through the materials and/or attend the seminars just like the regular paid park staff. It is a pain but it doesn't really take very long and you get credit in hours worked for completed them. Hey, a few less hours you have to work cleaning.

I am sure there are a lot of other downsides to volunteering but I just can't think of them right now. If you have some you would like added please get in touch with us and we will write an article about them. Go to our website: http://our-great-adventure.whatthehellblog.com/contact/ and use our Contact Form.

The Jobs

This book is about being a campground host. But there are other volunteer jobs in our Florida State Parks where you can get a FREE Campsite and we wanted to add those here as well. We have been sent general job descriptions for a number of the volunteer positions and are including them below. Not every park will have all of these duties and some of them will add more to them. It will depend on the individual park's needs and the time you are working for them. Remember, if you have any questions about your duties please ask the park's Volunteer Coordinator for clarification.

Below you will find Job Sheets about various volunteer jobs in our Florida State Parks that we have received from Hillsborough River State Park, Talbot Islands State Parks, Suwannee River Wilderness Trail and a few others over the last year. These are basic guidelines into the type of work that is asked of volunteers in exchange for the great benefits we receive for helping them.

Some are short and some are more detailed and formal looking. As with any job these are "general" duties that are expected of the volunteers assigned to these positions. Depending on your length of stay, time of year volunteering and the current situation at the park the jobs may be added to or taken away. They are a guideline and not necessarily set in stone. The park staff, volunteer coordinator and/or manager may need you to do other duties as well.

Basic Campground Host Job Description

Hillsborough River State Park

Campground Hosts are park ambassadors. They perform a variety of tasks such as greeting visitors and handing out information, replacing restroom supplies, cleaning campsites, picking up litter, and informing the rangers about potential problems. Hosts serve as official greeters and must like people, be courteous, outgoing, and helpful to all park visitors. Host volunteers need to be physically capable of performing these duties. You will be scheduled to work varied days and hours, not to exceed 32 hours per week. Hosts are asked to give full attention to their volunteer effort by not accepting employment outside the park during their stay as hosts. We ask for at least a 60 day commitment.

We supply campground hosts with:

Free camping with hookups and a sign for your campsite

A Volunteer Orientation Guidebook about Florida State Parks

A uniform designating your status as volunteer - consisting of a cap, t-shirts, and name tag

Training by State Park personnel

Insurance for job-related medical costs

Goal/Outcome of Job: Make guests feel welcome and keep campgound sites and restrooms clean and well maintained.

Supervisor: Assistant Park Manager or designee

Work location: Campground

Hours Required: Resident Volunteers: 5 days a week, (hours will vary with workload). We ask for a minimum of 20 hours/ week for one person and 32 hours/ week for a couple. There are usually 3 couples assigned campground host positions. Schedules can vary and overlap to suit individual desires or work-loads. A minimum of two-month commitment is required for this position and a maximum of 4 months is allowed.

Uniform: FPS Volunteer T-shirt with "black" trousers or shorts.

Duties and Responsibilities:

Hospitality: Make guests feel welcome by providing information and assistance while conveying a friendly, professional Florida Park Service image.

Camp Monitor: Be aware of park rules and regulations; have copies of same to be given out to campers who do not seem to be aware of them. Always approach campers in a kind and respectful manner. Notify a ranger of any problems in the campground that cannot be resolved in the above manner. Call a ranger to report disturbances during quiet hour (11:00 p.m.-8:00 a.m.).

Campground Facility Maintenance: Inspect restrooms periodically for cleanliness and to keep appropriate supplies well stocked.

Make repairs as needed - replace burned-out light bulbs, repair leaks, etc.

Report vandalism to your supervisor and clean or make repairs as necessary.

Report maintenance/repair needs that you cannot handle to your supervisor provide them with a written list.

Keep the outside of the building looking nice—sidewalks swept, and cobwebs and mud daubers removed.

For All Volunteer Positions Keep In Mind:

Volunteers are selected on a variety of factors. Experience is preferred but not required. We understand that a major draw for Volunteers is to learn new skills, see new places and meet new people. Do not let any perceived shortcoming in experience ever deter you from applying for a volunteer position in the Florida Park Service. After all, variety is the spice of life.

****

This is an excellent job sheet and describes the duties, benefits and requirements for most, if not all, the Campground Host positions in every Florida State Park. Below we have added a few more of the volunteer positions that some of the parks may need that do not involve working in a campground but will still get you a FREE Campsite in exchange for working.

Grounds Maintenance/Visitors Services

Hillsborough River State Park/Fort Foster Historic Site

Community/Resident Volunteer Program

Volunteer Program Goal: The Hillsborough River State Park/Fort Foster Historic Site will have a volunteer program that is manageable, efficient and does not exceed the Park's capacity to supervise effectively.

A Florida Park Service employee supervises all positions listed, and all positions work with a mix of Park Service employees and other volunteers. All positions require people who are self-motivated, have a strong work ethic, and the ability to work independently or in teams of 2 or more people.

Grounds Maintenance/Visitors Services

Position description: Duties include but are not limited to: Assisting with grounds maintenance and custodial duties at this state park. Assist park rangers in informing public about park rules and regulations; provide public assistance (first aid, CPR); etc. Cleanup of park facilities; park equipment; cleaning toilets; removing trash in recreation sites; patrols park on foot; assisting in the care and maintenance of any vehicles used for to perform duties. Making visitor contacts to answer questions; educate recreationists about the area. The volunteer will always present a neat, professional appearance and wear appropriate uniform components and name plate while working in the public eye and on official duty. This position requires a uniform t-shirt, which will be provided to you at no cost. Black work pants and appropriate black shoes are a requirement provided by the volunteer. The volunteer will always have a professional, courteous and helpful attitude when dealing with all members of the public, fellow volunteers and Park Service employees. The volunteer will be trained in and adhere to all Park Service Safety and Customer Service Procedures.

Goal/Outcome of Job: Assist with maintaining the park's grounds.

Supervisor: Assistant Park Manager or designee

Work location: Throughout the park.

Grounds Maintenance/Visitors Services *(Available Shifts Below)*

Hours Required: Resident Volunteers: minimum of 32 hours a week. A minimum of two-month commitment is required for this position and a maximum of 4 months is allowed.

Qualifications: 18 years or older; volunteer must complete and submit a Florida Park Service Volunteer Agreement Form; a search of the state's sexual predators and offender's registration information maintained by the Florida Department of Law Enforcement shall be conducted.

Required skills and abilities:

Standing and sitting for long periods

Light to moderate lifting, 15 – 50 lbs.

Must be physically able to work outdoors in varying weather conditions.

Familiar with common power tools.

A valid driver's license and good driving record

Other helpful (not required) skills and abilities:

Valid Red Cross First Aid and CPR certificate

For All Volunteer Positions Keep In Mind:

Volunteers are selected on a variety of factors. Experience is preferred but not required. We understand that a major draw for Volunteers is to learn new skills, see new places and meet new people. Do not let any perceived shortcoming in experience ever deter you from applying for a volunteer position in the Florida Park Service. After all, variety is the spice of life.

****

Toll Collector and Office Assistant

Talbot Islands State Parks

12157 Heckscher Drive

Jacksonville, FL 32226

(904 251-2320

Position: Ranger Station: Toll Collector and Office Assistant

Assigned Tasks: Assists Ranger Station staff at Little Talbot in the collection of daily usage fees. Assist with camper check in procedures and guidance. Answer phone calls and questions pertaining to a variety of topics about our park.

Supervisor: Assistant Park Managers and Volunteer Coordinator

Hours Required: Residency: 20 hours per week. At least 1-4 months per year are necessary.

Qualifications & Skills: Excellent public relations and communication skills. Toll collection and/or cash register experience are a plus but not required. Good writing and math skills. Basic computer skills are beneficial.

Standards & Performance: Must meet the minimum number of hours required each week. Must submit monthly log of hours worked each month. Must be able to present oneself in a professional manner to the public when encountered. Must be trained in and adhere to all Florida Park Service Safety and Customer Service Procedures and convey an understanding of our mission statement to the public and to fellow staff members. Must adhere to the volunteer uniform standards as designated by the supervisor. Must be able to work independently and with staff and other volunteers effectively.

****

Greeter/Docent

Talbot Islands State Parks

12157 Heckscher Drive

Jacksonville, FL 32226

(904 251-2320

Position: Greeter/Docent

Assigned Tasks: Greets park visitors at the Ribault Club on Fort George Island. Answers general questions and provides a brief introduction to the history of the Ribault Club.

Supervisor: Assistant Park Managers and Volunteer Coordinator

Hours Required: Residency - 32 hours per week. At least 1 to 4 months per year are necessary.

Qualifications & Skills: This position deals extensively with public interaction and providing visitor services. An outgoing personality, the ability to communicate professionally, and excellent public relation skills are beneficial. An interest in cultural resources and local history are helpful.

Standards & Performance: Must meet the minimum number of hours required each week. Must submit monthly log of hours worked each month. Must be able to present oneself in a professional manner to the public when encountered. Must be trained in and adhere to all Florida Park Service Safety and Customer Service procedures and convey an understanding of our mission statement to the public and to fellow staff members. Must adhere to the volunteer uniform standards as designated by supervisor. Must be able to work independently and with staff and other volunteers effectively.

****

One of our favorite places to volunteer is with the Suwannee River Wilderness Trail River Camps. Only canoers and kayakers are allowed to camp in these campgrounds but there are private outfitters who will drive into the camps and setup the area for a large group of paddlers coming in for the night. Each of the River Camps has one campground host who takes care of the entire camp by themselves. The Park Rangers or Manager will drive in supplies and take out the garbage when requested. They will also repair or arrange for the repair of anything that breaks if you are not able to do fix it yourself. Here is the ad that we responded to from one of the Workamper websites:

Volunteer Camp Host

Suwannee River Wilderness Trail

Florida State Parks Interested in volunteering at a Florida State Park? Our Park has 5 different River Camps which we manage, and we are seeking Camp Hosts for each of these River Camps for the coming spring, summer, and fall seasons. These camps are only assessable by River or hiking in (no vehicle access for park visitors). We do have full hook up including septic for our Campground host, and a washer/dryer (free to our host). You would need a RV or motor home.

These camps are for the most part in a remote part of the woods, and you would be out there by yourselves. You would basically be 'running' the camps for us. We do have rangers come in and do garbage pick-up and resupply, etc. We stay in contact with our hosts all the time – and you can call us any time you need us. At our camps we have 5 screened in platforms (16 x 16) with electric/water – and also primitive camping sites. There is a large pavilion, and restrooms. Right now we are not charging fees for these camps. Campers can only access these by river or hiking in – we do not allow anyone to drive in (with some exceptions for ADA).

The typical work week would require no more than 20 hours of actual physical work. The Camp Host off the clock presence on site is preferred as a deterrent to mischief makers. Days off are flexible. We do expect our hosts to work weekends that is our busy time. Weekdays can be on the slow side (with the exception of spring break). We do not mind if you need to take 'time off' (more than 12 hrs. outside of camp) we just need notice so we can have coverage for the camp. We have no problem with you leaving the camp during the week to run errands, etc.

Duties and responsibilities include:

1. Welcome visitors as appropriate. Record and report visitation (daily headcount). Accept and note visitor comments and suggestions while interpreting the wilderness trail concept and intended use to visitors.

2. Keeping facilities clean serviceable and operational in accordance with Chapter 15 of the Florida Park Service Operations Manual. To include but not limited to Maintaining cleanliness of:

Signs

Restrooms and showers

Sleeping platforms

Tables

Grills and fire rings

Sidewalks Stairs and Decks

Pick up litter camp wide, empty trash

Keep structures free of insect infestation mold and mildew

3. Monitor chlorine level in tank, test and record chlorine level of potable water twice weekly (staff will provide required training).

4. Mow and trim approved areas of camp (keeping in mind it is a wilderness camp not a garden park) Trim and maintain campsites, paths and platform areas.

5. In the rare event of river flooding Volunteer host will be required to assist staff with evacuation of equipment and disaster preparation of structures prior to evacuation as applicable and required.

6. Volunteer host should always keep safety in mind and practice safe work habits.

****

We enjoyed our volunteer experience so much we have come back for 4 months this time. You just never know what kinds of assignments, people or events you might come across when you are working for the Florida State Parks.

General Park Hosts

Bald Point State Park Host

Park volunteer will have a commitment of up to four months in a fiscal year, which is defined as beginning July 1st and continuing through to the end of the next June. Campsite will be assigned upon arrival. All keys will be issued upon arrival and returned upon departure. *All hosts are here solely at the discretion of the Park Services Specialist.*

Duties will include:

*Your work schedule will be provided to you upon arrival and is subject to change.

*Designated a <u>float position</u>, this individual will enjoy the diversity of various duties, and a various schedule based on park needs.

*Maintains and cleans the day-use area restrooms to a high level of sanitation and safety, and is responsible for nightly or when needed the emptying of the garbage receptacles throughout the park.

*Operates blowers to remove sand and storm runoff from around parking areas, sidewalks, entrances and all park drives.

*Responsible for maintaining grounds and facilities, debris and downed limb removal, as well as hazard reporting/resolution in the day use area which includes picnic tables and pavilions and surrounding areas, boat ramp, park drives and parking areas.

*Pick up of debris and trash along the North Point parking areas, frontage at both sides of park entrance and also along Range Road at the Chaires Creek entrance.

*Empty and clean Barbeque grills as required.

*To maintain clear views trim trees up to height as reachable with pruning loppers.

*Trim shrubbery to maintain aesthetics and safety of persons and property.

*Trim limbs which encroach upon roadways or pathways and trails.

*Mows and trims along park entrance drive, day-use road shoulders and common areas.

*The Ranger on duty may request additional duties as required due to need or circumstance.

*Is required to fill out daily fuel logs in vehicles after their closing shift.

*Follow all procedures on the Bald Point State Park Closing Procedure list that will be provide or located in any vehicle fuel log folder.

Park host are a vital part of day to day operations at Bald Point State Park. As a park host, you serve as the general visiting public's Ambassador and must have the ability to answer a variety of visitor's inquires in a thoughtful and courteous manner; and to tactfully advise (not enforce) and inform guests of the rules and regulations.

****

Maintenance Assistant Hosts

Bald Point Maintenance Assistant Host

Maintenance Assistant volunteer will have a commitment of an up to four months in a fiscal year, which is defined as beginning July 1st and continuing through to the end of the next June. Campsite will be assigned upon arrival. All keys will be issued upon arrival and returned upon departure. *All hosts are here solely at the discretion of the Park Manager.*

Duties will include:

*Your work schedule will be provided to you upon arrival and is subject to change.

*Designated a <u>float position</u>, this individual will enjoy the diversity of various duties, and a various schedule based on park needs.

*Primarily will be focused on the maintenance mechanic aspect of the equipment dealing with mechanical repairs, electrical installation and repair, plumbing installation and repair or building structure construction and repairs.

*May be called upon to perform the duties of Park Host in the event a temporary fill-in is required. May be assigned duties and assignments at another park or at off-park locations.

*This candidate should possess a working knowledge of electrical circuitry, plumbing systems, vehicle mechanics and construction.

*Will assist or conduct assignments such as mechanical repairs, electrical installation and repair, plumbing installation and repair or building structure repairs as required.

*Must demonstrate good safety practices, and will inspect and observe park grounds and structures for any safety hazards which may exist

*You will be required to keep the shop and work areas CLEAN, SAFE, And ORGANIZED and FREE FROM ANY SAFETY CONCERNS.

*An inherent ability to access situations and good problem solving skills are fundamental.

*This person should have the ability to operate machinery to include tractors, trucks, welders, torches and numerous power and hand tools.

*This individual should have the ability to handle an ever changing daily task schedule and to thrive on little "routine".

*Assist with all Park Special Events as needed.

*Must be able to answer visitor's inquiries, and possess good communication skills.

Maintenance Assistant host are a vital part of day to day operations at Bald Point State Park. By signing below you have read and agree to the above commitment and duties.

****

Park Zone Volunteer

Bahia Honda State Park

Position Description: Park Zone Volunteer

Hours: Three 8 hours shifts per week per volunteer site. Rotating weekends.

Time: 7:30 - 4:00

Bahia Honda State Park is divided into three work zones. Volunteers work three days in one zone and then rotate to another zone on the next scheduled 3 days.

Zone volunteers are responsible for the following:

*Cleaning of men's and women's restrooms once per day with several follow up visits throughout the day to ensure maintained cleanliness. Cleaning must be done to park standards and park specific procedures must be followed.

*Cleaning of campsites to include litter pick-up, cleaning of grills and light trimming of weeds and other vegetation as needed.

*Checking sites and informing camper check in station of status of site. This is to insure that all campers can check into a clean site as soon as possible.

*Emptying of all trash and recycling receptacles in the zones. This is done on a continuing basis throughout the day.

*Two of the zones have fish cleaning stations that need to be monitored and cleaned throughout the day.

*Two zones have beach walkways and pavilions that need to be cleared of sand at the start of each day. This is done with power blowers and or brooms.

*Monitoring, and picking up roads and use areas to ensure litter is not present throughout the day.

*It is the responsibility of the zone volunteer to correct any deficiencies or maintenance issues in the zone to which they are assigned, or to report said deficiency of maintenance issue to the Assistant Park Manager or person in charge on weekends.

*Zone volunteers are expected to know the rules and policies of the park and when infractions are noted handle politely or to report said infractions to uniformed staff.

*Cleaning and maintaining all equipment tools, and work areas used by the volunteer during the course of the day.

*Customer Service. Assist park visitors when possible, answer visitor question, Carry out all duties and interactions with guests in a polite, professional and most importantly a friendly manner.

****

Cabin Attendant Volunteers

Blue Springs State Park

Position Description: Cabin Attendant

Schedule: Cabin Attendant should be prepared to work 4-5 hours per day, preferably two to three days per week, for a total of at least 15 hours per week. Schedules for this position are necessarily somewhat loose and unstructured, since needs can arise at odd hours. In general, we would like Cabin Attendant to be on duty in the mornings by 11 am through check-out times, inspecting and maintaining the assigned area.

Responsibilities

Florida Park Service standards for *Cabin Attendant* are:

Cabin Attendants are responsible for the following:

1) Provide public relations and information.

2) Maintain cabins to Florida Park Service standards

3) Report deficiencies in the cabins to park staff for corrective action.

We intend to adapt these standards where possible to the Cabin Host position. Some more job-specific standards include:

Cabin Area cleaning

Police cabin loop area regularly. Remove litter and trash, empty trash cans and recycling containers. Police yards and driveways of unoccupied cabins, sweeping steps, cleaning grills, etc.

Cabin Occupancy, cleaning and laundry operation.

Get occupancy report from Ranger Station each morning each morning of duty. Verify proper occupancy and confirm with Ranger Station personnel. Coordinate activities with Cabin OPS or Park Ranger Assigned to cabins. Clean cabins per cabin cleaning standard after occupants check out, remove and launder linens, neatly fold cleaned linens, restock linens in cabins per reservation occupancy.

Inspection: Inspect tables, grills, and outside water service for safety and serviceability. Make minor repairs as possible; notify a staff member or the Assistant Park Manager of other problems as necessary. Notify the first available staff person immediately of any safety problems.

Patrol: Patrol the assigned area each day of duty. On this patrol, Hosts should familiarize themselves with cabin occupants as possible, condition of the cabins, possible behavior problems, and any safety issues. This is the opportunity to promote the public service image of the Florida Park Service by showing hospitality, answering questions, and providing information concerning the Park and the surrounding community.

Compliance with rules and regulations

Cabin Attendant should monitor activities in their assigned area, noting possible behavior problems, which could cause disorder or disturbance to other visitors. Cabin Attendant should report the cabin that is causing disturbances to others, <u>exercising the utmost in courtesy and good public relations</u>.

Cabin Attendant must always use an extreme amount of discretion in carrying out this responsibility. Cabin Attendant should never enter into any situation which is, or threatens to become, confrontational. When these situations are observed, call for assistance.

The Assistant Park Manager or Park Manager should only be called at home in the event of a facility emergency such as a fire, broken water main, or a tree fallen on a structure, etc. *The Assistant Park Manager and Park Manager are not law enforcement officers and cannot respond to law enforcement emergencies.* All law enforcement emergencies should be directed to the Florida Park Patrol and/or to the Sheriff's Department.

All volunteer employees should remember at all times that they are now agents of the Florida Park Service. The FPS has a unique, powerful image which we must all strive to honor and uphold. Most park visitors will view you as a Park Ranger. We will as well. Therefore, remember to maintain a high standard of public respect and friendliness, never be afraid to tell someone, "I'm sorry, I don't Know – but I'll find out for you" and lastly remember that our name is the Florida Park <u>SERVICE</u>!

****

Marina Host Volunteer Position

Hontoon Island State Park

Dock Master/Marina Host Position

This is an opportunity for self-motivated, hardworking, team player (individual or couple) to fill a resident Volunteer Dock master – Marina Host position at Hontoon Island State Park. The candidate (s) will be required to work independently with minimal supervision. Must have your own boat, water and electric is provided. There is a nearby marina to pump out as sewer is not included in this resident position. Must possess and maintain a Florida Class E driver's license. Must be able to successfully complete a background check. Must be willing to work weekends and Holidays. Must be able to fill the minimum 32 hr. work requirement.

POSITION DESCRIPTION: Maintains the cleanliness and function of the marina bathrooms, Assures cleanliness of grounds and facilities, works in the Island Store, provides customer service to park patrons, helps with general park maintenance.

****

River Guide Volunteer

Lake Griffin State Park

Position Description – Volunteer River Guide

Assigned Tasks: Prep & put away vessels and gear, visitor assistance, radio communication.

Number of Hours Required: 4 – 8 hours per week. Varies depending upon the schedule.

Examples of Work Performed:

* Gather life vests, paddles, whistles, and seats and bring to launch area before guests arrive.

* Unlock and remove vessels from storage racks. If applicable, attach seats to kayaks.

* Assist guests with life jacket adjustments and seating adjustments.

* Assist guests with getting into vessels and launching of vessels.

* Use of park radio. Notify the ranger station to report the total number of people departing.

* If necessary, help guests with navigational questions and/or on the water paddling instruction.

* If necessary, helping guests that have capsized their vessels or are in need of first aid.

* Paddle up to 3 miles roundtrip through the Dead River Marsh and into Lake Griffin.

* Lead the way for guests as the paddle trip leader or keep the group together as the "sweep."

* Assist guests with getting out of vessels.

* Return vessels to storage racks and lock vessels.

* Return all life vests, paddles, whistles and seats to storage shed/ranger station.

* Work with all visitors, volunteers and staff in a helpful and professional manner.

* Answer general questions about the Florida Park Service and/or Lake Griffin State Park.

Knowledge Skills and Abilities:

* Knowledge of the geography of the Dead River and Lake Griffin.

* Skilled at paddling canoes and/or kayaks.

* Ability to lift a canoe or a kayak with the help of one other person.

* Ability to work independently and under supervision.

* Ability to work in difficult environmental conditions with factors such as extreme heat, rain or insects.

* Ability to follow and retain both verbal and written instructions.

* Ability to interpret, understand and apply rules, regulations, policies and procedures.

* Ability to establish and maintain effective working relationships with others.

* Ability to navigate through the Dead River Marsh and paddle up to 3 miles.

Training/Pre-Requisite: CPR / AED / First Aid Certification required. Experience paddling canoes or kayaks required. DEP Certification in canoe & kayak safety required. Knowledge of interpretive techniques, Florida ecosystems, plants, and animals preferred.

Updated 4/2014

****

Below is a Volunteer Duty Description Sheet that was sent to us via email from the Volunteer Coordinator at Troy Springs State Park where we will be Resident Hosts next summer.

Residential/Park Hosts

Troy Springs State Park

Position Title: Park Host (2 positions available)

Service Availability: Immediately (each for a service period of 6 to 16 weeks)

Minimum Service Hours Required: Individual - 20 hours/week Couple -32 hours/week

Weekly Work Schedule: 4-5 days on, 2-3 days off, based on season and staff availability. Specific times and days TBD.

Assigned Duties & Responsibilities: (duties vary based on need, season, and availability)

Visitor Services: Follow proper park opening and closing procedures; answer visitor questions or locate relevant information and resources; answer office phone as necessary; greet guests and provide consistent quality and friendly customer service. Additional opportunities may be available including interpretive programming, interpretive signage/content development, and event/program coordination.

Maintenance: Clean/check restroom daily using minimum cleaning restroom standards established by park and adhere to proper Personal Protective Equipment (training provided during orientation) for all on-duty activities; perform park maintenance, trail maintenance, and basic landscaping. Additional opportunities may be available including electrical, plumbing, carpentry, mechanical maintenance, and watercraft operation.

Resource Management: Record river level and rain gauge levels daily; record observed wildlife; assist in the identification and treatment/removal of exotic and/or invasive plant species (requires additional training); assist in the identification and monitoring of cultural/archaeological resources (requires additional training). Additional opportunities may be available including plant and animal inventories, as well as imperiled species surveying and monitoring.

Administration: Check mail; perform clerical tasks such as filing, organizing, photocopying, etc. Additional opportunities may be available including graphic design, digital photography, as well as data entry.

Protection: Assist FPS employees with the voluntary enforcement of all park policies and DEP Directives, including payment of entrance fees.

Preferred Knowledge/Skills Preferred

Camp Host or other volunteer experience with the Florida Park Service, National Park Service, any county, city or non-Florida park, non-profit or for-profit organization, etc.

Customer Service/Visitor Services experience in retail, food service industry, hospitality, etc.

Experience in custodial work, sanitation, industrial hygiene, and/or knowledge of OSHA/ANSI standards, etc.

Mechanical, electrical, plumbing, carpentry, small engines, and/or general knowledge of hand tools, power tools, etc.

Experience as a docent, interpreter, guide, educator, and/or training as a Master Naturalist, Master Gardener, or similar certification.

Certification in Fist Aid, CPR, AED and/or first responder, emergency response, fire fighter, etc.

Some proficiency in kayaking/canoeing or water vessel w/outboard motor operation.

Current Driver's License (minimum: Class E)

Benefits to Volunteers

In exchange for meeting minimum number of service hours required, volunteer will receive a full hook-up (water, electric, and septic) site free-of-charge for up to 16 weeks (service period depends on park's need and availability);

In exchange for meeting minimum number of service hours required, volunteer will be permitted to utilize park facilities and amenities, free-of-charge for the duration of his/her service.

At 100 service hours, volunteer will receive a Volunteer ID card which permits the volunteer's immediate family free entry into the park of current service at no-charge;

At 500 service hours, volunteer will become eligible to apply for and receive a Special Volunteer Annual Pass, which permits the volunteer and up to 7 other guests (per 1 vehicle) into most Florida state parks free-of-charge;

Uniform materials will be made available to volunteer at the beginning of service as re-supplied as necessary/available;

All regular-service Volunteers are covered under state liability protection (Section 768.28, F.S.) and by Workers' Compensation (Chapter 440, F.S.);

Invitation to Florida Park Service Volunteer events and socials; eligibility for recognition and nomination through the Volunteer Recognition Program;

Training opportunities (inside and outside the FPS);

Additional benefits may include but are not limited to: improved physical, emotional and psychological health; increased knowledge and skill-sets; gaining friendships and camaraderie amongst other volunteers, staff, and guests; improved level of safety, condition, and overall function of the park, while maintaining the mission of the Florida Park Service.

Uniform & Safety Requirements

All Volunteers are required to comply with all uniform and safety requirements, as established by the park of service, the Florida Park Service, and the Florida Department of Environmental Protection. All uniform and safety requirements will be addressed during the mandatory Volunteer Orientation, which usually takes place within the first week of service.

Expectations & Performance

All Volunteers are expected to comply with all rules, policies, and standards established by the park of service, the Florida Park Service, and the Florida Department of Environmental Protection. All Volunteers are subject to a 2-week probationary period at the beginning of his/her service.

We will be Park/Camp Hosts at Troy Springs State Park next year. We do not meet all the requirements listed in this duty sheet so they can be a little flexible. This park is fairly small with just a spring pool, picnic tables, trails and a bathroom. It is very popular with divers, swimmers as well those kayaking or canoeing down the Suwannee River. The only problem is that the Suwannee River has been overflowing a lot in the last couple of years and the attendance in the park has been greatly affected. The Park Services Specialist/Volunteer Coordinator who signed us up for this volunteer assignment will not be there next year. Hopefully, the next person will be just as nice and enthusiastic about putting this small place on everyone's "Must Visit" list.

****

Our final Volunteer Duties Description Sheet is from another of our future volunteer assignments at St. Sebastian River Preserve State Park:

North Camp Area Volunteer Responsibilities

St Sebastian River Preserve

Volunteer Responsibilities

North Camp Area

Prior to acceptance all volunteers must complete a Florida State Parks volunteer application, background check, and all state required training as a part of the volunteer orientation process.

Responsibilities

In exchange for a free campsite, camp volunteers are expected to perform the following duties: (Some duties are shared daily/weekly with other volunteers)

*Close gate every night at Sunset, check trash/recycles at spillway and lock restroom at visitor center (VC). (Shared duty)

*Open gate every day at 8am and unlock restroom at visitor center. Clean as needed. (Shared duty)

*Work the visitor center as per scheduling (Fri – Sat, 10 to 430 & Sun 12 - 430) (Shared duty)

*Respond to campers' questions regarding the Preserve, camping rules and locations of local businesses, etc.

*Make sure each camper obtains a camping permit from the Preserve office prior to camping and that appropriate payment has been made.

*Mow and weed-eat as needed:

***Parking lots

***Shop compound

***Camp sites

***Camp Host area

*Pick up trash along roadways

*Check camp sites (clean out fire pits and pick up trash)

*Check Shop (sweep and take out trash)

*Clean visitor center and North Office (weekday visitor center) each week (restrooms, Vacuum carpets and take trash to dumpster) (Shared duty)

*Trail maintenance (may require operation of heavy machinery)

*Miscellaneous projects to be assigned

Terms of assignment

All Volunteers:

*Are required to perform a minimum of 20 hours of service every week

*Will turn in a timesheet at the end of each quarter with hours served

*May only give camper code (<u>not staff code</u>) to patrons who are left in park after hours so they may exit (if approved through a park staff member first)

*Will use authorized vehicles only on service roads and trails and will check/fill fluids and clean vehicles after each use

Please Note- Volunteer privileges can be revoked at any time at the discretion of park management. Your mailing address will be 1000 Buffer Preserve Dr. Fellsmere, FL 32948

****

When you accept an assignment or even when you inquire about volunteering at any of the Florida State Parks you can ask the Volunteer Coordinator to send you a copy of the Job Duties for each of the volunteer positions you are considering. They can email it to you so that you can read through them to make sure you understand what they are asking of their volunteers and you can discuss anything you have a question about or a problem doing.

Each of these positions had to have had a Job Duties and/or Description Sheet created that was approved by the Park Manager and District Park Manager. You are supposed to be able to read them before you sign as a volunteer. Remember that these are general descriptions and you can be asked to do more or less duties while you are there. After all, you are there to help the park and the park staff. Should you have any questions about any additional duties please discuss them with the Volunteer Coordinator or whichever park staff assigned you the duties. The park staff should make sure you are trained to do whichever assignments you are given and that you are comfortable doing them. This includes being trained to use their equipment, machines and tools required to get the jobs done.

New Live On-Site Volunteers Considerations

If you haven't figured it out by now almost every single Florida State Park has more than enough volunteers for the winter months when all the "Snowbirds" come down. Conversely, over two-thirds of the Florida State Parks needs volunteers in the late spring through the early to mid-fall months. Summer time is always the hardest to get people to volunteer at the inland areas.

The parks and management areas located on the Atlantic Ocean, the Gulf of Mexico and in the Florida Keys don't have as many problems getting volunteers during the summer months. So, these state parks are harder to get volunteer assignments at any time of the year. If you have your heart set on volunteering at any of these parks you will have to contact each one personally to make sure your application is on file. Then you will, more than likely, have to be very flexible about when you will volunteer. Most of these parks will contact you at the last minute when one of the "regular" volunteers cannot come. As far as we know these parks do not limit the number of years volunteers can return only that they put in their request before they finish their current assignment to return the next year. So far, we have only found one Florida State Park that placed a "3 Years in a row" limit on returning volunteers.

The only limits that the Florida Department of Environmental Protection (Agency that runs the Florida State Parks) has placed on the Florida State Parks Volunteer program is that volunteers can only stay a maximum of 4 months at any one park during the fiscal year (July to June) without express permission from the District Park Manager. Those exceptions are generally only given for someone with a specialized skill needed to finish a park project. And, possibly some of the inland state parks that really need volunteers to stay all through the late spring to the end of summer.

The other Florida county parks, national parks, national forests, Florida forests, Water Management Districts and Wildlife Management Areas have their own requirements, length of stay limitations volunteer handbooks and amenities for volunteers. See their page below for their information and where, if available, online you can get more information about their programs, amenities and requirements.

For those considering Florida State Parks their Volunteer Handbook is available to you online to read more about the program. It is available for download directly from the volunteer page on the Florida State Parks website. http://www.floridastateparks.org/getinvolved/volunteer.cfm

Things to Consider Before Applying at any Florida Park

Only you can decide if you want to volunteer at a particular park. You might want to keep in mind a few things when considering any one of them.

Is this park somewhere I want to spend a few months at?

Can I commit the length of time they are asking me to do?

Can I do the duties that they are asking me to do while I am volunteering?

Am I willing to be at this park during the time of year they are asking me to serve?

If you have never been to the park you are considering there are lots of online resources to find out more information about the park and the general area around the park. We recommend reading through the information on the park's webpages, searching through the videos on You-Tube taken at the park and asking some fellow Full-Time RVers if they have volunteered there before and what they experienced while there.

Volunteer Timesheet Info

There is a lot of paperwork that needs to be filled out before you start any new volunteer assignment with Florida State Parks just as there is some paperwork that will need to be done during your assignment as well. One of the most important one is the Time Sheet Form. The following descriptions are given to help you decide where to put the hours you have work

Administration

The term ADMINISTRATION refers to clerical work, filing, answering the telephone, certain types of research, tracking volunteer hours, orientation and training, data entry, purchasing, grant writing or tracking, etc.

Maintenance

The term MAINTENANCE refers to upkeep, repairs and improvements to facilities, equipment and grounds, carpentry, trail maintenance, plumbing, masonry, painting, preventative maintenance, mowing, trash pick-up, restroom upkeep, vehicle and equipment maintenance, small engine work, electrical work, construction projects, etc.

Protection

The term PROTECTION refers to visitor safety, employee safety, emergency preparedness, emergency response, law enforcement, rule enforcement, voluntary compliance, facility and environmental protection, First Aid, CPR, state/vehicle watercraft operation, etc.

Resource Management

The term RESOURCE MANAGEMENT includes both natural and cultural resources and refers to exotic species Identification and control, plant and animal identification, ecological or cultural restoration, prescribed fire, lake watch, species monitoring, seed collecting, historical collections management, research, etc.

Visitor Services

The term VISITOR SERVICE refers to providing information and access, customer service, interpretation, docent, historical and re-enactment, assisting visitors in the ranger station or visitor center, tram rides, concessions, special events, boat tours, educational programs, guided walks, public speaking, volunteer management, visitor program evaluations, etc.

THIS information and much more is located in the Florida State Parks Volunteer Handbook available for download directly from their website

Florida State Parks with Live On-Site Volunteers

The Florida State Parks are divided into Districts which represent different regions of the State. These are District 1 – Northwest Region, District 2 – Northeast Region, District 3 – Central Region, District 4 – Southwest Region and, District 5 – Southeast Region. Each has their own District Park Manager, and District Volunteer Coordinator assigned. The District Park Manager is in charge of each of the Park Managers and the District Volunteer Coordinator will send applications to the parks within their region for consideration. Then the park's Volunteer Coordinator will contact the applicants directly.

Below we have included the district number next to the park name but listed the parks in alphabetically order. You can download a Florida State Parks Book directly from the website and it includes a map of Florida divided into regions and parks listed within the district.

It should be noted that some parks have campground hosts only, some have residential or park hosts only and some have both. Campground Hosts have campsites in the campground, whereas, the Park/Residential Hosts are generally placed in a Volunteer Village located at or near the parks shop area. These campsites are generally reserved for the volunteers who have mechanical, carpentry, or other skills needed behind the scenes as it were, including maintaining trails, working in the ranger station, cleaning the "day-use" areas, etc. The campground hosts are there to keep the campground area and buildings cleaned, the area mowed and trimmed and assist the campers.

We originally collected this information into an Excel spreadsheet. If you would like me to send you a copy of the spreadsheet to aid in your own volunteering research please contact me directly via email: our-great-adventure@whatthehellblog.com

We offer this spreadsheet for FREE to anyone who has bought our book as a bonus!

Alafia River State Park – District 4

Ronald Stevens - Park Ranger, Volunteer Coordinator

14326 South County Road 39

Lithia, FL 33547

(813) 672-5320

Ronald.Stevens@dep.state.fl.us

http://www.floridastateparks.org/alafiariver/

No of Campground Host Positions: 2

Campsite Amenities: Water, Electric and Dump station

Electric Types: 20/30/50Amps

RV/Trailer Length Limits: 60'

Tent or Boat Camping: none

No. of Park/Residential Hosts: 5

Campsite Amenities: Water, Electric, Sewer

Electric Types: 20/30/50Amps

RV/Trailer Length Limits: 60'

FREE Extras: Washer/Dryer and Firewood

Other Amenities/Notes: Monthly Volunteer Social and Yearly party end of March

Hours Required: 20 hours per week for Singles; 32 hours per week for Couples

Length of Stay: 2 to 4 months

Example of Jobs/Duties: Camp Host; Maintenance; Ranger Station

Times Volunteers Needed Most: Late Spring into early Fall.

Alfred B Maclay Gardens State Park - District 1

Elizabeth H Weidner, Resident Park Manager II

3540 Thomasville Road

Tallahassee, FL 32309

(850) 487-4115

elizabeth.weidner@dep.state.fl.us

http://www.floridastateparks.org/maclaygardens/default.cfm

Number of Campground Hosts: 0

No. of Park Hosts Positions: 2

Campsite Amenities: Water/Electric/Sewer

Electric Types: 30/50Amp

RV/Trailer Rig Length Limits: none

FREE EXTRAS: laundry

Other Park Amenities/Notes: None

Hours Required: 24 off Season/32 Peak Season

Length of Stay: 1 to 4 months - 3 years in a row only

Examples of Duties: Docents in house museum or visitor center, (Jan-Apr) or may perform maintenance duties including cleaning restrooms

Times Volunteers Needed Most: Summer

Anastasia State Park - District 3

Brittany C Sims McDermott, Park Services Specialist/Volunteer Coordinator

1340-A A1A South

St. Augustine, FL 32080

(904) 461-2000

brittany.sims@dep.state.fl.us

http://www.floridastateparks.org/anastasia/default.cfm

No. of Campground Hosts: 8

Campsite Amenities: Water/Electric/Sewer

Electrical Types: 30Amps

RV/Trailer Rig Length Limit: 40'

Tent and/or Boat Camping: none

No. of Park/Residential Hosts: 0

Free Extras: Washer/Dryer

Other Park Amenities/Notes: None

No. of Hours Required: 20 hours per week

Length of Stay: 2 to 4 weeks

Examples of Duties: Campground Hosts, Facilities Maintenance, Special Projects

Times Volunteers Needed Most: Summer and December

Bahia Honda State Park - District 5

Brittany Burtner, Park Services Specialist/Volunteer Coordinator

36850 Overseas Hwy

Big Pine Key, FL 33043

(305) 782-3897

brittany.burtner@dep.state.fl.us

http://www.floridastateparks.org/bahiahonda/default.cfm

No. of Campground Hosts: 4

Campsite Amenities: Water/Electric with Dump Station

Electrical Types: One is 20/30Amp - 2 are 20/30/50Amp

RV/Trailer Rig Length Limits: 1 is Tent or Small Popup/3 the rest 45'

Tent or Boat Camping: yes

No. of Park/Residential Hosts: 4

Campsite Amenities: Water/Electric/Sewer

Electrical Types: 30Amp

RV/Trailer Rig Length Limit: 45'

FREE Extras: Ice Machine/Washer & Dryer/Extra Freezers

Other Park Amenities/Notes: NEW POSITION - 1 Boat Park Host with Water/30Amp and Septic Pump-Out

Hours Required: 24 Hours per Week

Length of Stay: 3 to 4 months

Examples of Duties: Campground Duties; Facilities Maintenance; Grounds Maintenance; Ranger Station

Times Volunteers Needed Most: None

Bald Point State Park – District 1

Dustin L Allen, Park Services Specialist/Volunteer Coordinator

146 Box Cut

Alligator Point, FL 32346

(850) 962-2771

Dustin.L.Allen@dep.state.fl.us

http://www.floridastateparks.org/baldpoint/default.cfm

No. of Campground Hosts: 0

Tent and/or Boat Camping: none

No. of Residential/Park Hosts: 2 – More depending on needs

Campsite Amenities: Water/Electric/Sewer

Electrical Types: 30Amp

RV/Trailer Rig Length Limits: 40'

FREE Extras: Laundry/Extra Shower/Fridge/Freezer/Ice Machine

Other Park Amenities/Notes: poor cellphone or TV reception but good satellite reception

Hours Required: 20 Hour per week

Length of Stay: 2 to 4 months

Example of Duties: Facilities Maintenance, Grounds Maintenance, Customer Service

Times Volunteers Needed Most: Late Spring to Early Fall

Big Lagoon State Park - District 1

Kiersten Wilson, Park Services Specialist/Volunteer Coordinator

12301 Gulf Beach Highway

Pensacola, FL 32507

(850) 492-1595

Kiersten.L.Wilson@dep.state.fl.us

http://www.floridastateparks.org/biglagoon/default.cfm

No. of Campground Hosts: 3

Campsite Amenities: Water/Electric and a Dump Station

Electrical Types: 30/50Amp

RV/Trailer Rig Length Limit: 40'

Tent and/or Boat Camping: Tent possible (check to confirm)

No. of Resident/Park Hosts: 3

Campsite Amenities: Water/Electric and a Dump Station

Electrical Type: 30/50Amp

RV/Trailer Rig Length Limit: 40'

FREE Extras: Boat Ramp, Kayak and Canoes

Park Amenities/Notes: This Park is near enough to Pensacola you can receive a couple of TV channels with just a Digital Antennae and cellphone reception is excellent.

Hours Required: 20 hours per week

Length of Stay: 1 to 4 months

Example of Duties: Campground Hosts and Maintenance Host Duties

Times Volunteers Needed Most: None

Big Shoals State Park- District 2

Gary A Erixton, Park Ranger

11330 S.E. County 135

White Springs, FL 32096

(386) 397-2733

gary.erixton@dep.state.fl.us

http://www.floridastateparks.org/bigshoals/default.cfm

No. of Campground Hosts: 0

No. of Park/Resident Hosts: 1

Campsite Amenities: Water/Electric with a dump station

Electrical Type: 50Amp

RV/Trailer Rig Length Limit: None

FREE Extras: none

Other Park Amenities/Notes: Use of Facilities after park closes

Hours Required: 20 hours per week

Length of Stay: 2 to 4 months

Examples of Duties: Facilities Maintenance, Grounds Maintenance, Trail Maintenance, Cleaning, Opening and Closing the park

Times Needed Volunteers Most: Late Spring to Early Fall

Blackwater River State Park – District 1

Marshall Shaw, Park Services Specialist/Volunteer Coordinator

7720 Deaton Bridge Rd

Holt, FL 32564

(850) 983-5363

marshall.a.shaw@dep.state.fl.us

http://www.floridastateparks.org/blackwaterriver/default.cfm

No. of Campground Hosts: 1

Campsite Amenities: Water/Electric/Sewer

Electrical Types: 30/50Amp

RV/Trailer Rig Length Limit: None

Tent or Boat Camping: Tents possible, Confirm with park

No. of Residential/Park Hosts: 2

Campsite Amenities: Water/Electric/Sewer

Electrical Types: 30/50Amp

RV/Trailer Rig Length Limit: 45'

FREE Extras: Laundry

Other Park Amenities/Notes: Terrible Cellphone Reception

Hours Required: 25 Hours a Week

Length of Stay: 2 to 4 months

Example of Duties: cleaning campsites, cleaning bathrooms, general facility maintenance, trail maintenance, building maintenance, interpretation, administration.

Times Volunteers Needed Most: Summer Months

Blue Spring State Park – District 3

Laura L Kruger, Park Services Specialist/Volunteer Coordinator

2100 West French Avenue

Orange City, FL 32763

(386) 775-3663

laura.kruger@dep.state.fl.us

http://www.floridastateparks.org/bluespring/default.cfm

No. of Campground Hosts: 2

Campsite Amenities: Water/Electric with a Dump Station

Electrical Types: 30/50AMPS

RV/Trailer Rig Length Limit: None

Tent/Boat Camping: None

No. of Residential/Park Hosts: 2

Campsite Amenities: Water/Electric/Sewer

Electrical Types: 20/30Amps

RV/Trailer Rig Length Limit: None

FREE Extras: laundry

Other Park Amenities/Notes: None

Hours Required: 20 Hours a Week

Length of Stay: 2 to 4 months

Examples of Duties: Campground Duties, cabin attendant, interpretation, maintenance (grounds and repairs), tollbooth attendant and various other projects

Times Volunteers Needed Most: Late Spring and Summer Months

Caladesi Island State Park - District 4

Karen A Malo, Park Services Specialist/Volunteer Coordinator

#1 Causeway Blvd

Dunedin, FL 32720

(386) 736-5309

karen.malo@dep.state.fl.us

http://www.floridastateparks.org/caladesiisland/default.cfm

No. of Campground/Marine Hosts: 4

Campsite Amenities: Water/Electric

Electrical Type: Shore Power

Camping Rig Limits: Boats Only-40'x12'

Tent or Boat Camping: Boat Camping Only

No. Residential/Park Hosts: 0

FREE Extras: None

Other Park Amenities/Notes: Island only accessible via boat. Has Shore Power and Potable Water Supply

Hours Required: 20 Hours per Person

Length of Stay: 2 to 4 months

Example of Duties: Facilities Maintenance, Checking in Boat Campers

Times Volunteers Needed Most: Summer

Camp Helen State Park - District 1

Daniel Burton, Park Services Specialist/Volunteer Coordinator

23937 Panama City Beach Pkwy

Panama City Beach, FL 32413

(850) 233-5059

Daniel.Burton@dep.state.fl.us

http://www.floridastateparks.org/camphelen/default.cfm

No. of Campground Hosts: 0

No. Residential/Park Hosts: 2

Campsite Amenities: Water/Electric/Sewer

Electrical Types: 30/50Amp

RV/Trailer Rig Length Limit: None

FREE Extras: laundry

Other Park Amenities/Notes: Poor Cellphone reception

Hours Required: 20 Hours a Week

Length of Stay: 2 to 4 months

Example of Duties: residential host positions, general duties include cleaning bathrooms, projects, maintain grounds mowing, edging, weed eating etc. Projects, Events, and customer service, anything the park needs.

Times Volunteers Needed Most: Summer Months

Cayo Costa State Park - District 4

Zachary Lozano, Park Services Specialist/Volunteer Coordinator

P.O. Box 1150

Boca Grande, FL 33921

(941) 964-0375

Zachary.Lozano@dep.state.fl.us

http://www.floridastateparks.org/cayocosta/default.cfm

No. of Campground Hosts: 5

Campsite Amenities: primitive tent sites with shower house

Electrical Types: none

RV/Trailer Rig Length Limit: tent sites only

No. of Residential Hosts: 0

FREE Extras: Volunteers get free rides on the Ranger Boat to and from Island

Other Park Amenities/Notes: Contact: Mary Olsen 239-633-1654 for more information about the island and volunteering there. The Island is only accessible via water.

Hours Required: 20 Hours

Length of Stay: As Little as a few days up to 4 months

Example of Duties: Facilities Maintenance; Visitors Center; Tram Driver; Wood Work; Exotic Plant Removal

Times Volunteers Needed Most: Summer Months

Cedar Key Museum State Park/Waccasassa Bay Preserve - District 2

Christopher Camargo, Park Services Specialist/Volunteer Coordinator

12231 SW 166 Court

Cedar Key, FL 32625

(352) 543-5567

christopher.camargo@dep.state.fl.us

http://www.floridastateparks.org/cedarkeymuseum/default.cfm

http://www.floridastateparks.org/waccasassabay/

No. of Campground Hosts: 0

No. of Residential/Park Hosts: 2

Campsite Amenities: Water/Electric with Dump Station

Electric Type: 30Amp

RV/Trailer Rig Length Limit: 35'-40'

FREE Extras: None

Other Park Amenities/Notes: Site is located at Waccasassa Bay Preserve, good cellphone service, quiet and relatively private, water is mostly non-potable

Hours Required: 20 hours per week

Length of Stay: 2 to 4 months

Example of Duties: Museum Docents

Times Volunteers Needed Most: Summer Time

Collier-Seminole State Park - District 4

Kirby Wilson/Darren L Flickinger, Park Manager/Park Services Specialist

20200 E. Tamiami Trail

Naples, FL 32625

(352) 543-5567

kirby.wilson@dep.state.fl.us and darren.flickinger@dep.state.fl.us

http://www.floridastateparks.org/collierseminole/default.cfm

No. of Campground Hosts: 4

Campsite Amenities: Water/Electric and a Dump Stations

Electrical Types: Call for Current Amp Types

RV/Trailer Rig Length Limit: None

No. of Residential/Park Hosts: 11

Campsite Amenities: Water/Electric/Sewer

Electrical Types: Call for Current Amp Types

RV/Trailer Rig Length Limit: None

FREE Extras: Laundry/Ice machine/Range/Oven

Other Park Amenities/Notes: Campsites currently going through renovations beginning in May 2014 for next 12 months or so. You need to contact the park directly to find out if any volunteers are needed and what campsite amenities are currently available

Times Volunteers Needed Most: Summer Months

Curry Hammock State Park - District 5

Robert F Rose, Park Ranger/Volunteer Coordinator

56200 Overseas Hwy

Marathon, FL 33050

(305) 289-2690

robert.rose@dep.state.fl.us

http://www.floridastateparks.org/curryhammock/default.cfm

No. of Campground Hosts: 2

Campsite Amenities: Water/Electric and a dumping station

Electrical Types: 20/30/50Amp

RV/Trailer Rig Length Limits: 45'

No. of Residential/Park Hosts: 2

Campsite Amenities: Water/Sewer/Electric

Electrical Types: 20/30/50Amps

RV/Trailer Rig Length Limits: 45'

FREE Extras: washer and dryer

Other Park Amenities/Notes: none

Hours Required: 20 to 30 hours per week

Length of Stay: 2 to 4 months

Examples of Duties: campground restroom cleaning, day use restroom cleaning, campsite cleaning, recycling collection, mowing, tree trimming, odd jobs

Times Volunteers Needed Most: June to September

Dade Battlefield Historic State Park - District 4

Kristin N Wood, Park Ranger/Volunteer Coordinator

7200 County Road 603

Bushnell, FL 33513

(352) 793-4781

Kristin.N.Wood@dep.state.fl.us

http://www.floridastateparks.org/dadebattlefield/default.cfm

No. of Campground Hosts: 0

No. of Residential/Park Hosts: 3

Campsite Amenities: Water/Electric/Sewer

Electrical Types: 15/30/50Amps

RV/Trailer Length Limit: 50'

FREE Extras: Laundry/Shower/Extra Refrigerator and Freezer

Other Park Notes/Amenities: None

Hours Required: 20 hours per week

Length of Stay: 2 to 4 months

Example of Duties: Facilities Maintenance; Toll Booth; Grounds Maintenance; Event Helpers and Pioneer Craft Demonstrators

Times Volunteers Needed Most: Late Spring to Early Fall

De Leon Springs State Park - District 3

Donna L Collins, Park Services Specialist/Volunteer Coordinator

601 Ponce Deleon Blvd

Deleon Springs, FL 32130

(386) 985-4212

donna.collins@dep.state.fl.us

http://www.floridastateparks.org/deleonsprings/default.cfm

No. of Campground Hosts: 0

No. of Residential/Park Hosts: 2

Campsite Amenities: Water/Electric/Sewer

Electric Type: 30Amps

RV/Trailer Rig Length Limits: None

FREE Extras: laundry

Other Park Amenities/Notes: None

Hours Required: 20 Hours a Week

Length of Stay: 2 to 4 months

Examples of Duties: Restroom cleaning, mowing, weed eating, blowing, painting, litter pick-up and working on projects throughout the park

Times Volunteers Needed Most: June to September

Delnor-Wiggins Pass State Park - District 4

Donna Young, Park Services Specialist/Volunteer Coordinator

11135 Gulf Shore Dr. N.

Naples, FL 34108

(239) 593-2658

Donna.Young@dep.state.fl.us

http://www.floridastateparks.org/delnorwiggins/default.cfm

No. of Campground Hosts: 0

No. of Residential/Park Hosts: 1

Campsite Amenities: Water/Electric/Sewer

Electrical Type: 30Amp

RV/Trailer Rig Length Limit: None

FREE Extras: Washer/Dryer at Shop

Other Park Amenities/Notes: None

Hours Required: 20 Hours a Week

Length of Stay: 3 Months

Example of Duties: Duties Vary by Skill of Volunteer and Needs of Park Staff

Times Volunteers Needed Most: Summer

Dr. Julian G Bruce St George Island - District 1

Melody C Brennan, Park Services Specialist/Volunteer Coordinator

1900 E. Gulf Beach Dr.

St. George Island, FL 32328

(850) 927-2111

melody.brennan@dep.state.fl.us

http://www.floridastateparks.org/stgeorgeisland/default.cfm

No. of Campground Hosts: 2

Campsite Amenities: Water/Electric and a Dump Station

Electrical Types: 30/50Amp

RV/Trailer Rig Length Limit: 42'

No. of Residential/Park Hosts: 4

Campsite Amenities: Water/Electric and a Dump Station

Electrical Types: 30/50Amp

RV/Trailer Rig Length Limit: 42'

FREE Extras: Free Canoe/kayak rentals, Ice Machine

Other Park Amenities/Notes: Poor Cellphone and TV antennae reception but excellent satellite reception

Hours Required: 20 hours per week

Length of Stay: 2 to 4 months

Examples of Duties: Campground Host, Maintenance Duties; Grounds Duties; Ranger Station

Times Volunteers Needed Most: Summer Months

Dudley Farm Historic State Park - District 2

Sandra Cashes, Park Services Specialist/Volunteer Coordinator

18730 W. Newberry Rd

Newberry, FL 32669

(386) 454-4201

Sandra.Cashes@dep.state.fl.us

http://www.floridastateparks.org/dudleyfarm/default.cfm

No. of Campground Hosts: 0

No. of Residential/Park Hosts: 2

Campsite Amenities: Water/Electric/Sewer

Electrical Types: 30Amp

RV/Trailer Rig Length Limit: 40'

FREE Extras: Free vegetables out of the garden

Other Park Amenities/Notes: Hoping to add 2 more sites in the future

Hours Required: 20 hours per week

Length of Stay: 2 to 4 months

Example of Duties: Facilities Maintenance; Grounds Maintenance; helping with the chicken coops and feeding; historic and vegetable garden maintenance; fence repair; chicken coop repair; cleaning inside the historic buildings

Times Volunteers Needed Most: Call the Park for More Information

Econfina River State Park – District 1

Theresa C. Messler, Park Services Specialist/Volunteer Coordinator

County Road 14 South

Econfina, FL 32336

(850) 922-6007

Terri.messler@dep.state.fl.us

http://www.floridastateparks.org/econfinariver/default.cfm

No. of Campground Hosts: 0

No. of Residential/Park Hosts: call park for more information

Campsite Amenities: Water/Electric/Sewer

Electrical Type: 30/50Amp

RV/Trailer Rig Length Limit: None

FREE Extras: washer/dryer

Other Park Amenities/Notes: Access to Gulf, great fishing, poor cellphone and TV antennae reception but good satellite reception

Hours Required: 20 hours per week minimum

Length of Stay: 2 to 4 months

Example of Duties: call park for more information

Times Volunteers Needed Most: generally during the summer months

Eden Gardens State Park - District 1

Daniel Burton, Park Services Specialist/Volunteer Coordinator

181 Eden Gardens Rd

Santa Rosa Beach, FL 32459

(850) 233-5058

Daniel.Burton@dep.state.fl.us

http://www.floridastateparks.org/edengardens/default.cfm

No. of Campground Hosts: 0

No. of Residential/Park Hosts: 2

Campsite Amenities: Water/Electric/Sewer

Electrical Type: 30/50Amp

RV/Trailer Rig Length Limit: None

FREE Extras: laundry

Other Park Amenities/Notes: Access to canoes

Hours Required: 20 Hours per Week

Length of Stay: 2 to 4 Months

Example of Duties: Residential host positions, general duties include cleaning bathrooms, projects, maintain grounds mowing, edging, weed eating etc. Projects, Events, and customer service, anything the park needs.

Times Volunteers Needed Most: Summer Months

Edward Ball Wakulla Springs State Park - District 1

Jacqueline M. Turner, Park Services Specialist/Volunteer Coordinator

465 Wakulla Park Drive

Wakulla Springs, FL 32327

(850) 561-7276

Jackie.m.turner@dep.state.fl.us

http://www.floridastateparks.org/wakullasprings/default.cfm

No. of Campground Hosts: only has cabins

No. of Residential/Park Hosts: 4

Campsite Amenities: Water/Electric/Sewer

Electrical Types: 20/30/50Amps

RV/Trailer Rig Length Limits: 40'

FREE Extras: Washer and Dryer, Free River Boat Tours

Other Park Amenities/Notes: None

Hours Required: 20 hours per week per person

Length of Stay: 2 to 4 months

Example of Duties: Work in Ranger Station collecting entrance fees and greeting visitors, facility maintenance, special projects

Times Volunteers Needed Most: Summer months

Fakahatchee Strand Preserve State Park - District 4

Melissa A. Miano, Park Ranger/Volunteer Coordinator

137 Coastline Dr.

Copeland, FL 34137

(239) 695-4593

melissa.miano@dep.state.fl.us

http://www.floridastateparks.org/fakahatcheestrand/default.cfm

No. of Campground Hosts: 0

No. of Residential/Park Hosts: 5

Campsite Amenities: Water/Electric/Sewer

Electrical Types: 30/50Amps

RV/Trailer Rig Length Limits: None

FREE Extras: Washer/Dryer/Ice Machine/Water Filters

Other Park Amenities/Notes: Campfire Ring, Canoe & Kayaks

Hours Required: 20 hours per week

Length of Stay: 2 to 4 months

Examples of Duties: Resource Management, Maintenance and Visitor Services - from clearing trails, mowing, cleaning grounds, helping in ranger station and interpretive guides depending on volunteers skills and interests and the needs of the park at the time of service.

Times Volunteers Needed Most: Summer time

Falling Waters State Park - District 1

Scott A Sweeney, Park Services Specialist/Volunteer Coordinator

1130 State Park Rd

Chipley, FL 32428

(850) 638-6130

scott.sweeney@dep.state.fl.us

http://www.floridastateparks.org/fallingwaters/default.cfm

No. of Campground Hosts: 2 to 4 Depending on Needs

Campsite Amenities: Water/Electric/Sewer

Electrical Types: 30/50Amp

RV/Trailer Rig Length Limits: 45'

No. of Residential Hosts: 0

FREE Extras: Laundry, Ice, Firewood

Other Park Notes/Amenities: None

Hours Required: 20 to 24 hours per week

Length of Stay: 2 to 4 months

Examples of Duties: Ranger Station, cleaning of facilities, mowing, different maintenance jobs requiring carpentry, plumbing, painting and landscaping skills.

Times Volunteers Needed Most: Summer Months

Fanning Springs State Park - District 2

Anthony (Kirk) Marhefka, Park Services Specialist/Volunteer Coordinator

18020 N.W. Hwy 19

Fanning Springs, FL 32693

(352) 535-5181

Kirk.Marhefka@dep.state.fl.us

http://www.floridastateparks.org/fanningsprings/default.cfm

No. of Campground Hosts: 0

No. of Residential/Park Hosts: 1

Camping Amenities: Water/Electric/Sewer

Electrical Types: 30Amps

RV/Trailer Rig Length Limits: 41'

FREE Extras: None

Other Park Amenities/Notes: Poor Cellphone Service

Hours Required: 20 hours per week

Length of Stay Required: 2 to 4 months

Examples of Duties: Ranger Station, Maintenance, Grounds, Cabin Rentals After Hours

Times Volunteers Needed Most: Early Spring to Early Fall

Faver-Dykes State Park - District 3

Dennis Pope, Park Services Specialist/Volunteer Coordinator

1000 Faver Dykes Rd

St. Augustine, FL 32086

(904) 794-0097

dennis.pope@dep.state.fl.us

http://www.floridastateparks.org/faverdykes/default.cfm

No. of Campground Hosts: 1

Campsite Amenities: Water/Electric/Sewer

Electrical Types: 30Amps

RV/Trailer Rig Length Limit: 35'

No. of Residential/Park Hosts: Varies with Needs and abilities - Contact Park Directly

Campsite Amenities: Water/Electric and a dump station – staying in campground

Electrical Types: 30AMPs

RV/Trailer Rig Length Limit: 35'

FREE Extras: laundry, Firewood, Ice

Other Park Amenities/Notes: Poor Cellphone Service, access to boat launch

Hours Required: 20 Hours per week

Length of Stay: 2 to 4 months (willing to negotiate time as little as a week for those with maintenance skills, carpentry, etc. depending on needs)

Examples of Duties: Campground Host Duties and assist Park Rangers

Times Volunteers Needed Most: Summer time mostly – contact park directly to make other arrangements depending on your skills and their needs at the time

Florida Caverns State Park - District 1

Billy Bailey, Park Services Specialist/Volunteer Coordinator

3345 Caverns Rd

Marianna, FL 32446

(850) 482-1228

William.Bailey@dep.state.fl.us

http://www.floridastateparks.org/floridacaverns/default.cfm

No. of Campground Hosts: 2

Campsite Amenities: Water/Electric/Sewer

Electrical Types: 30/50Amp

RV/Trailer Rig Length Limits: 45'

No. of Residential Hosts: 4

Campsite Amenities: Water/Electric/Sewer

Electrical Types: 30/50Amp

RV/Trailer Rig Length Limits: 45'

FREE Extras: Showers, Laundry, Firewood, Ice

Other Park Amenities/Notes: Park Has Equestrian Camping Area, Spring Swimming and Fishing Area

Required Hours: 40 hours per week per campsite

Length of Stay: 1 to 4 months

Example of Duties: Park host duties depend on the position, positions include Maintenance/cleanup, Cave tour guide, Rangers station, Nature exhibit, and Ticket sales

Times Volunteers Needed Most: Summer

Fort Clinch State Park - District 2

Marie Buche, Park Services Specialist/Volunteer Coordinator

2601 Atlantic Ave

Fernandina Beach, FL 32034

(904) 277-7274

Marie.Bucher@dep.state.fl.us

http://www.floridastateparks.org/fortclinch/default.cfm

No. of Campground Hosts: 2

Campsite Amenities: Water/Electric and a Dump Station on Beach Side; Sewer on River Side

Electrical Type: 30Amp

RV/Trailer Rig Length Limit: 40'

No. of Residential/Park Hosts: 6

Campsite Amenities: Water/Electric/Sewer

Electric Types: 30/50Amp

RV/Trailer Rig Length Limits: 45'

FREE Extras: Volunteer Bath house, laundry and ice machine

Other Park Amenities/Notes: Shared Laundry Ask for small donation to CSO, limited cellphone service at some of the campsites

Hours Required: 20 hours per week

Length of Stay: 1 to 4 months

Examples of Duties: Campground Duties; Facilities Maintenance; Grounds Maintenance; Ranger Station

Times Volunteers Most Needed: Summer Months

Fort Cooper State Park - District 2

Dianne Drye, Park Ranger/Volunteer Coordinator

3100 South Old Floral City Rd

Inverness, FL 34450

(352) 726-0315

dianne.drye@dep.state.fl.us

http://www.floridastateparks.org/fortcooper/default.cfm

No. of Campground Hosts: 0

No. of Residential/Park Hosts: 2

Campsite Amenities: Water/Electric/Sewer

Electrical Types: 30Amp

RV/Trailer Rig Length Limit: 30 to 45'

FREE Extras: laundry; communal freezer and fridge

Other Park Amenities/Notes: None

Hours Required: 20 hours per week

Length of Stays: 3 to 4 months

Examples of Duties: park facilities maintenance, grounds maintenance

Times Volunteers Needed Most: Late Spring through Early Fall

Fort George Island Cultural State Park - District 2

Brian Stinson, Park Ranger/Volunteer Coordinator

12157 Heckscher Dr.

Jacksonville, FL 32226

(904) 251-2324

Brian.Stinson@dep.state.fl.us

http://www.floridastateparks.org/fortgeorgeisland/default.cfm

No. of Campground Hosts: 0

No. of Residential/Park Hosts: 1

Campsite Amenities: Water/Electric/Sewer

Electrical Type: 30Amps

RV/Trailer Rig Length Limits: 35'

FREE Extras: none

Other Park Amenities/Notes: We have Volunteer House with 3 bedrooms that is shared with volunteers that do not have campers for Ribault Center

Hours Required: 20 hours per week

Length of Stay: 2 to 4 months

Example of Duties: Museum Docent

Times Volunteers Needed Most: Summer Months

Fort Pierce Inlet State Park – District 5

Lisa Phillips, Park Services Specialist/Volunteer Coordinator

905 Shorewinds Dr

Fort Pierce, FL 34949

(772) 468-3985

Lisa.phillips@dep.state.fl.us

http://www.floridastateparks.org/fortpierceinlet/default.cfm

No. of Campground Hosts: 0

No. of Residential Hosts: 2

Campsite Amenities: Water/Sewer/Electric

Electrical Types: 50Amp

RV/Trailer Rig Length Limits: 40'

FREE Extras: Washer/Dryer

Other Park Amenities/Notes: None

Hours Required: 24 hours/Single, 32 hours couple per week

Length of Stay: 2 to 4 months

Examples of Duties: Volunteer duties vary from visitor services to field projects. Visitor services primarily involves working at the Ranger Station. Volunteers scheduled to work the Ranger Station greet park visitors, collect entrance fees, sell annual passes, process pavilion reservations, use a credit card machine, disperse park information, give directions etc. Field projects involve assisting the rangers in the field. Duties may include, but are not limited to: opening and closing the park entrance gates, emptying garbage bins, cleaning restrooms, cleaning barbeque grills, recording water meter readings, picking up litter, trail maintenance, general park maintenance etc.

Times Volunteers Needed Most: Late spring to early fall

Fort Zachary Taylor Historic State Park - District 5

Rebecca Rabe, Park Services Specialist/Volunteer Coordinator

601 Howard England Way

Key West, FL 33040

(305) 292-6713

Rebecca.Rabe@dep.state.fl.us

http://www.floridastateparks.org/forttaylor/default.cfm

No. of Campground Hosts: 0

No. of Residential/Park Hosts: 4

Campsite Amenities: Water/Electric/Sewer

Electrical Type: 30/50Amp

RV/Trailer Rig Length Limits: 40'

Other Park Amenities/Notes: Laundry for Monthly Fee, Ice, Wi-Fi

Hours Required: 20 hours per week

Length of Stay: 2 to 4 months

Example of Duties: Grounds Maintenance; Facilities Maintenance; Toll Collectors; Special Projects

Times Volunteers Needed Most: Summer Time can sometimes be a problem

Fred Gannon Rocky Bayou State Park - District 1

Katrina Synder (Kit), Park Services Specialist/Volunteer Coordinator

4281 State Road 20 East

Niceville, FL 32578

(850) 650-5928

Katrina.e.hamilton@dep.state.fl.us

http://www.floridastateparks.org/rockybayou/default.cfm

No. of Campground Hosts: call for more information

Campsite Amenities: Water/Electric/Sewer

Electrical Types: 30/50Amp

RV/Trailer Rig Length Limits: 40'

No. of Residential Hosts: call for more information

Campsite Amenities: Water/Sewer/Electric

Electrical Types: 30/50Amp

RV/Trailer Rig Length Limits: 40'

FREE Extras: Washer/Dryers/Ice

Other Park Amenities/Notes: None

Hours Required: 20 hours per week minimum, more as needed

Length of Stay: 2 to 4 months

Examples of Duties: campground duties, assisting rangers, ranger station duties, special projects

Times Volunteers Needed Most: sometimes during the summer months

Gamble Rogers Memorial State Recreation Area at Flagler Beach - District 3

Jennifer A Giblin, Park Services Specialist/Volunteer Coordinator

3100 South A1A

Flagler Beach, FL 32136

(386) 517-2086

jennifer.giblin@dep.state.fl.us

http://www.floridastateparks.org/gamblerogers/default.cfm

No. of Campground Hosts: 1 summer months; 2 during peak season

Campsite Amenities: 1 with Water/Electric/Sewer and 1 with just Water/Electric and use of dump station

Electrical Types: 30/50AMPS

RV/Trailer Rig Length Limits: None

No. of Residential Hosts: 3

Campsite Amenities: Water/Electric/Sewer

Electrical Types: 30/50AMPS

RV/Trailer Rig Length Limits: None

FREE Extras: Firewood/Washer & Dryer

Other Park Amenities/Notes: Use of canoes, kayaks and bicycles when not in use by visitors

Hours Required: 20 hours minimum, more when required

Length of Stay: 2 to 4 months

Examples of Duties: Regular campground host duties, assist the park rangers, ranger station duties, special projects

Times Volunteers Needed Most: None   really, call for more information

Grayton Beach State Park - District 1

Patrick W Hartsfield, Park Services Specialist/Volunteer Coordinator

357 Main Park Rd

Santa Rosa Beach, FL 32459

(850) 267-8300

patrick.w.harstfield@dep.state.fl.us

http://www.floridastateparks.org/graytonbeach/default.cfm

No. of Campground Hosts: 2

Campsite Amenities: Water/Electric/Sewer

Electrical Types: 30/50Amps

RV/Trailer Rig Length Limits: 35'

No. of Residential Hosts: 3

Campsite Amenities: Water/Electric/Sewer

Electrical Types: 30/50Amps

RV/Trailer Rig Length Limits: 35'

FREE Extras: None

Other Park Amenities/Notes: Coin Laundry located in campground

Hours Required: 20 hours per week minimum may do more depending on park needs

Length of Stay: 1 month to 4 months

Examples of Duties: Campground Hosts, Cabin Cleaners, Facilities Maintenance, Ranger Station, Special Projects

Times Volunteers Needed Most: May to September

Henderson Beach State Park - District 1

Lynda A. Smith, Park Services Specialist/Volunteer Coordinator

17000 Emerald Coast Pkwy

Destin, FL 32541

(850) 650-5928

Lynda.a.smith@dep.state.fl.us

http://www.floridastateparks.org/hendersonbeach/default.cfm

No. of Campground Hosts: call for more information

Campsite Amenities: Water/Electric with Dump Station

Electrical Types: 30/50Amp

RV/Trailer Rig Length Limits: 55'

No. of Residential Hosts: call for more information

Campsite Amenities: Water/Electric with Dump Station

Electrical Types: 30/50Amp

RV/Trailer Rig Length Limits: 55'

FREE Extras: Washer/Dryer/Ice

Other Park Amenities/Notes: None

Hours Required: 20 Hours per week minimum, more when required

Length of Stay: 2 to 4 months

Examples of Duties: Campground Host Duties, assist park rangers, ranger station duties, special projects.

Times Year Volunteers Needed Most: sometimes during the summer months

Highlands Hammock State Park - District 4

Carla Kappmeyer-Sherwin, Park Services Specialist/Volunteer Coordinator

5931 Hammock Rd

Sebring, FL 33872

(941) 386-6094

carla.kappmeyer-sherwin@dep.state.fl.us

http://www.floridastateparks.org/highlandshammock/default.cfm

No. of Campground Hosts: 6

Campsite Amenities: Water/Electric and a Dump Station

Electrical Types: 30Amp

RV/Trailer Rig Length Limits: 3 Sites 40 to 45' and 3 Sites 35'

No. of Residential/Park Hosts: 1 Reserved for Mechanic Helpers and others for OPS and special duties volunteers

Campsite Amenities: Water/Electric/Sewer

Electrical Types: 30Amps

RV/Trailer Rig Length Limits: 45'

FREE Extras: Laundry/Firewood

Other Park Amenities/Notes: Concessions and Recreation Hall

Hours Required: 20 hours per week

Length of Stay: 2 to 4 months

Examples of Duties: Regular Campground Host duties, facilities Maintenance, grounds-keeping helpers and ranger station assistants.

Time of Year Volunteers Needed the Most: April to September

Hillsborough River State Park - District 4

Alex Kinder, Park Services Specialist/Volunteer Coordinator

15402 U.S. 301 North

Thonotosassa, FL 33592

(813) 987-6870

douglas.kinder@dep.state.fl.us

http://www.floridastateparks.org/hillsboroughriver/default.cfm

No. of Campground Hosts: 4

Campsite Amenities: Water/Electric and a Dump Stations

Electrical Types: 30/50Amp

RV/Trailer Rig Length Limits: 50'

Tent Camping: Possible to Camp host in a Tent, Call to Confirm

No. of Residential/Park Hosts: 11

Campsite Amenities: Water/Electric/Sewer

Electrical Types: 30/50Amp

RV/Trailer Rig Length Limit: 50'

FREE Extras: Fire Ring, Picnic Table and Laundry

Other Park Amenities/Notes: Concessions/Swimming Pool, Rec Hall, Canoes

Hours Required: 20 hours per week

Length of Stay: 2 to 4 months (Offers to do 2 Weeks Trial Position in the summer with Option to extend for 2 Months)

Examples of Duties: Camp Host; Facilities Maintenance; Grounds Maintenance; Ranger Station

Times Volunteers Needed Most: Late Spring to Early Fall

Honeymoon Island State Park - District 4

Karen A Malo, Park Services Specialist/Volunteer Coordinator

#1 Causeway Blvd

Dunedin, FL 34698

(727) 469-5942

karen.malo@dep.state.fl.us

http://www.floridastateparks.org/honeymoonisland/default.cfm

No. of Campground Hosts: 0

No. of Residential/Park Hosts: 3

Campsite Amenities: Water/Electric/Sewer

Electrical Types: 30/50Amp

RV/Trailer Rig Length Limit: 40'

FREE Extras: Washer/Dryer

Other Park Amenities/Notes: Concessions

Hours Required: 20 per person

Length of Stay: 2 to 4 months

Examples of Duties: Facilities Maintenance; Toll Booth; grounds maintenance; equipment maintenance

Times Volunteers Needed Most: Summer Months

Hontoon Island State Park - District 3

Christine Garrett, Park Services Specialist/Volunteer Coordinator

2309 River Ridge Rd

Deland, FL 32720

(386) 736-5309

Christine.Garrett@dep.state.fl.us

http://www.floridastateparks.org/hontoonisland/default.cfm

No. of Campground Hosts: 1

Campsite Accommodations: They have small Trailer with Electric, Bunk Bed, Fridge, Microwave and AC with Have Bathhouse for water and Showers

No. of Boat Camp hosts: 1

Campsite Amenities: Water/Electric - No Sewer - Boat Slip

Electrical Type: Shore Power

FREE Extras: Free Ferry rides on and off the Island

Hours Required: 20 hours per week

Length of Stay: 6 weeks to 16 weeks

Examples of Duties: Facilities Maintenance, Ferry Driver, Boat Camp Host, Customer Service

Times Volunteers Most Needed: Late spring to fall

Hugh Taylor Birch State Park - District 5

Mark Edward Foley, Park Services Specialist/Volunteer Coordinator

3109 East Sunrise Blvd

Fort Lauderdale, FL 33304

(954) 468-2791

mark.foley@dep.state.fl.us

http://www.floridastateparks.org/hughtaylorbirch/default.cfm

No. of Campground Hosts: 0

No. of Residential Hosts: 6

Campsite Amenities: Water/Electric/Sewer

Electrical Types: 30/50Amp

RV/Trailer Rig Length Limits: none

FREE Extras: none

Other Park Amenities/Notes: none

Hours Required: 40 Hours per week

Length of Stay: 2 to 4 months

Examples of Duties: Toll Collecting Assistant; Youth Camp Lodge/Cabin Attendant (checking groups in/out, tending to facilities); Youth Primitive Camp Attendant (checking groups in/out, tending to facilities); Grounds Attendant (mowing/weed-eating); Resource Management Attendant (removal of exotic & Invasive species); Shop Assistant (maintenance skills required)

Times Volunteers Most Needed: April to September

Ichetucknee Springs State Park - District 2

Samuel A Cole, Park Services Specialist/Volunteer Coordinator

12087 SW US Hwy 27

Fort White, FL 32038

(386) 497-4690

Sam.Cole@dep.state.fl.us

http://www.floridastateparks.org/ichetuckneesprings/default.cfm

No. of Campground Hosts: 0

No. of Residential/Park Hosts: 2

Campsite Amenities: Water/Electric/Sewer

Electrical Types: 30/50Amps

RV/Trailer Rig Length Limits: 45'

FREE Extras: Laundry

Other Park Amenities/Notes: Working on Adding a 3rd site

Hours Required: 30 hours per week

Length of Stay: 2 to 4 months

Examples of Duties: During the summer tubing season (Memorial Day weekend through Labor Day), we are looking primarily for volunteers to assist with visitor services and transportation. Outside of tubing season, primarily openers and closers, Education Center docents, and Ranger Station assistance.

Times Volunteers Most Needed: Summer

John D. MacArthur Beach State Park - District 5

Lu E Dodson, Park Services Specialist/Volunteer Coordinator

10900 State Road 703 (A1A)

North Palm Beach, FL 33408

(561) 624-6950

lu.dodson@dep.state.fl.us

http://www.floridastateparks.org/macarthurbeach/default.cfm

No. of Campground Hosts: 0

No. of Residential Hosts: 2

Campsite Amenities: Water/Electric/Sewer

Electrical Types: 1-30Amp, 1-50Amp

RV/Trailer Rig Length Limits: 36'

FREE Extras: Laundry

Other Park Amenities/Notes: Our sites are located in the shop yard of the park, it is fenced in and locked at night. May use park dock, and get a 10% discount in the gift shop on most items

Hours Required: 30 Hours per week

Length of Stay: 2 to 4 months

Examples of Duties: Residential volunteers are at liberty to pick from a list of available volunteer positions that are open in the park when they are in residence. Educational programs, Nature Center Docent, Nature Walk guide, Gift Store Volunteer, Tram driver, Maintenance, etc. Residents are expected to help fill in on short notice when necessary.

Times Volunteers Most Needed: The summer/fall months are the hardest to fill: May through October.

John Pennekamp Coral Reef State Park - District 5

Elena Maria Muratori, Park Services Specialist/Volunteer Coordinator

U.S. 1 Mile Marker 102.5

Key Largo, FL 33037

(305) 451-1202

elena.muratori@dep.state.fl.us

http://www.floridastateparks.org/pennekamp/default.cfm

No. of Campground Hosts: call for information

Campsite Amenities: Water/Electric/Sewer

Electrical Types: 30/50Amp

RV/Trailer Rig Length Limits: 40'

No. of Residential Hosts: Call for information

Campsite Amenities: Water/Electric/Sewer/

Electrical Types: 30/50Amp

RV/Trailer Rig Length Limits: 40'

FREE Extras: None

Other Park Amenities/Notes: You will have to contact the Volunteer Coordinator with your questions

Hours Required: 20 hours per week minimum, more when necessary

Length of Stay: State Mandates 2 to 4 Months

Examples of Duties: call for more information

Times Volunteers Most Needed: Volunteer Coordinator states she is always booked year-round

Jonathan Dickinson State Park - District 5

Martin D Morse, Park Services Specialist/Volunteer Coordinator

16450 SE Federal Hwy.

Hobe Sound, FL 33455

(561) 744-9814

martin.morse@dep.state.fl.us

http://www.floridastateparks.org/jonathandickinson/default.cfm

No. of Campground Hosts: 8

Campsite Amenities: Water/Electric/Sewer - one site doesn't have sewer

Electrical Types: Some 30Amp but most 50Amp

RV/Trailer Rig Length Limits: None

No. of Residential/Park Hosts: 6

Campsite Amenities: Water/Electric/Sewer

Electrical Types: Some 30Amp but most 50Amp

RV/Trailer Rig Length Limits: None

FREE Extras: Laundry

Other Park Amenities/Extras: Volunteer Coordinator will be retiring soon will need to contact park directly for new Coordinator's Name and Email address.

Hours Required: 24 Hours per Week per campsite

Length of Stay: 2 to 4 months

Examples of Duties: Campground Host Duties, cleaning, trimming, mowing, maintenance,

Times Volunteers Needed Most: Good Quality volunteers harder to find during off season

Kissimmee Prairie Preserve State Park - District 3

Natalie S Carlson, Administrative Assistant/Volunteer Coordinator

33104 NW 192 Ave

Okeechobee, FL 34972

(863) 462-6360

natalie.carlson@dep.state.fl.us

http://www.floridastateparks.org/kissimmeeprairie/default.cfm

No. of Campground Hosts: 2

Campsite Amenities: Water/Electric and a Dump Station

Electrical Types: 30/50AMPS

RV/Trailer Rig Length Limits: 30' & 40'

No. of Residential/Park Hosts: 6

Campsite Amenities: Water/Electric with a Dump Station

Electrical Types: 30/50AMPS

RV/Trailer Rig Length Limits: 30' & 40'

FREE Extras: Laundry and Ice

Other Park Amenities/Notes: None

Hours Required: 20 hours per week

Length of Stay: 2 to 4 months

Examples of Duties: Campground Hosts, Facilities Maintenance, Groundskeeper, Ranger Station

Times Volunteers Needed Most: summer months

Koreshan State Historic Site - District 4

Michael M Heare, Park Services Specialist/Volunteer Coordinator

P.O. Box 7

Estero, FL 33928

(239) 992-0311

michael.heare@dep.state.fl.us

http://www.floridastateparks.org/koreshan/default.cfm

No. of Campground Hosts: 2

Campsite Amenities: Water/Electric and a Dump Station

Electrical Types: 30Amp

RV/Trailer Rig Length Limit: 40'

Tent Camping: possible check with Coordinator

No. of Residential/Park Hosts: 20

Campsite Amenities: Water/Electric/Sewer on 17 of 20 Sites

Electrical Types: 30Amp

RV/Trailer Rig Length Limits: 40'

FREE Extras: Canoe and Kayak Available for Volunteers

Other Park Amenities/Notes: Rec Hall with 2 Refrigerators and Coin Operated Laundry

Hours Required: 20 hours per week

Length of Stay: 2 to 4 months

Examples of Duties: Camp Hosts; Facilities Maintenance; Grounds Maintenance; Office Assistance; Gardening;

Times Volunteers Needed Most: Late Spring to Early Fall

Lafayette Blue Springs State Park - District 2

Larry W. Arrant, Park Services Specialist/Volunteer Coordinator

799 N.W. Blue Springs Rd

Mayo, FL 32066

(386) 294-3667

larry.arrant@dep.state.fl.us

http://www.floridastateparks.org/lafayettebluesprings/default.cfm

No. of Campground Hosts: 0

No. of Residential/Park Hosts: 4

Campsite Amenities: Water/Electric/Sewer

Electrical Types: 30/50Amps

RV/Trailer Rig Length Limits: 45'

FREE Extras: Laundry

Other Park Amenities/Notes: None

Hours Required: 20 hours per week

Length of Stay: 2 to 4 months

Examples of Duties: Grounds Maintenance; Facilities Maintenance; River Campground Host; Cabin Cleaners

Times Volunteers Needed Most: Late spring to early fall

Lake Griffin State Park - District 3

Doug Watson, Park Manager/Volunteer Coordinator

3089 US Highway 441-27

Fruitland Park, FL 34731

(352) 360-6760

doug.watson@dep.state.fl.us

http://www.floridastateparks.org/lakegriffin/default.cfm

No. of Campground Hosts: 2

Campsite Amenities: Water/Electric/Sewer

Electrical Types: 30/50Amps

RV/Trailer Rig Length Limit: 40'

No. of Residential/Park Hosts: 4

Campsite Amenities: Water/Electric/Sewer

Electrical Types: 30/50AMPS

RV/Trailer Rig Length Limit: 40'

FREE Extras: Laundry and Ice

Other Park Amenities/Notes: None

Hours Required: 30 hours per week

Length of Stay: 4 months

Examples of Duties: Park maintenance, interpretation, ranger station, toll collection, camper registration, reception, and park / equipment maintenance.

Times Volunteers Needed Most: Late spring to early fall.

Lake Jackson Mounds Archaeological State Park - District 1

Theresa C. Messler, Park Services Specialist/Volunteer Coordinator

3600 Indian Mounds Rd

Tallahassee, FL 32303

(850) 922-6007

Terri.messler@dep.state.fl.us

http://www.floridastateparks.org/lakejackson/default.cfm

No. of Campground Hosts: 0

No. of Residential Hosts: call park for more information

Campsite Amenities: Water/Electric/Sewer

Electrical Types: 50Amp

RV/Trailer Rig Length Limits: None

FREE Extras: Washer/Dryer/Shower

Other Park Amenities/Notes: Access to Tallahassee; good TV, satellite and cell service; topography and access challenges

Hours Required: 20 hours per minimum, more may be required as needed

Length of Stay: 2 to 4 months

Examples of Duties: call the park for more information

Times Volunteers Most Needed: summer months, generally

Lake Kissimmee State Park - District 3

Andrea L. (Andi) Henry, Park Services Specialist/Volunteer Coordinator

14248 Camp Mack Rd

Lake Wales, FL 33898

(863) 696-1112

andrea.henry@dep.state.fl.us

http://www.floridastateparks.org/lakekissimmee/default.cfm

No. of Campground Hosts: 2

Campsite Amenities: Water/Electric/Sewer

Electrical Type: 30AMPs

RV/Trailer Rig Length Limits: None

No. of Residential/Park Hosts: 2

Campsite Amenities: Water/Electric/Sewer

Electrical Type: 30AMPs

RV/Trailer Rig Length Limits: None

FREE Extras: Free Ice

Other Park Amenities/Notes: None

Hours Required: 20 hours per week

Length of Stay: 1 to 4 months

Examples of Duties: Cleaning Park Facilities, Grounds Maintenance, Customer Service

Times Volunteers Needed Most: Summer Months

Lake Louisa State Park - District 3

Jenny Vogel Kehlenbeck, Park Service Specialist/Volunteer Coordinator

7305 U.S. Highway 27

Clermont, FL 34714

(352) 394-3436

jenny.kehlenbeck@dep.state.fl.us

http://www.floridastateparks.org/lakelouisa/default.cfm

No. of Campground Hosts: 2

Campsite Amenities: Water/Electric/Sewer

Electrical Types: 20/30/50AMPS

RV/Trailer Rig Length Limit: None

No. of Residential/Park Hosts: 0

FREE Extras: Laundry

Other Park Amenities/Notes: Trying to get Cabin Cleaner Assistant Position and Camp Site Created

Hours Required: 20 Hours per week

Length of Stay: 2 to 4 months

Examples of Duties: Regular Campground Host Duties, grounds maintenance, customer service

Times Volunteers Needed Most: Summer Months

Lake Manatee State Park - District 4

Eduardo Alaniz, Park Ranger/Volunteer Coordinator

20007 State Road 64

Bradenton, FL 34212

(941) 741-3028

eduardo.x.alaniz@dep.state.fl.us

http://www.floridastateparks.org/lakemanatee/default.cfm

No. of Campground Hosts: 2

Campsite Amenities: Water/Electric and a Dump Station

Electrical Types: 30/50Amp

RV/Trailer Rig Length Limit: 50'

Tent Camping - Possible check with Volunteer Coordinator

No. of Residential/Park Hosts: 2

Campsite Amenities: Water/Electric/Sewer

Electrical Types: 30/50Amp

RV/Trailer Rig Length Limit: 50'

FREE Extras: Ice machine, Laundry

Other Park Amenities/Notes: Use of Any Rental Equipment like Canoes and Bikes

Hours Required: 20 hours per week

Length of Stay: 2 to 4 months

Examples of Duties: Camp Hosts; Facilities Maintenance; Grounds Maintenance; Ranger Station

Times Volunteers Needed Most: Late spring to early fall

Lake Talquin State Park - District 1

Theresa C. Messler, Park Services Specialist/Volunteer Coordinator

14850 Jack Vause Landing Rd

Tallahassee, FL 32310

(850) 922-6007

Terri.messler@dep.state.fl.us

http://www.floridastateparks.org/laketalquin/default.cfm

No. of Campground Hosts: 0

No. of Residential Hosts: call park for more information

Campsite Amenities: Water/Electric/Sewer

Electrical Types: 30/50Amp

RV/Trailer Rig Length Limits: None

FREE Extras: Washer

Other Park Amenities/Notes: Great freshwater fishing and boating; good TV and satellite service; poor cell service

Hours Required: 20 hours per week minimum, more may be required

Length of Stay: 2 to 4 months

Examples of Duties: call the park for more information

Times Volunteers Most Needed: possibly during the late spring to early fall months

Little Manatee River State Park - District 4

Jose Santiago, Park Ranger/Volunteer Coordinator

215 Lightfoot Rd

Wimauma, FL 33598

(813) 671-5005

jose.santiago@dep.state.fl.us

http://www.floridastateparks.org/littlemanateeriver/default.cfm

No. of Campground Hosts: 2

Campsite Amenities: Water/Electric and a Dump Station

Electrical Type: 30Amp

RV/Trailer Rig Length Limit: 40'

Tent Camping: Possible check with Coordinator

No. of Residential/Park Hosts: 5

Campsite Amenities: Water/Electric/Sewer

Electrical Type: 30amp

RV/Trailer Rig Length Limits: 40'

FREE Extras: Washer/Dryer at Shop

Other Park Amenities/Notes: None

Hours Required: 20 hours per week

Length of Stay: 2 to 4 months

Examples of Duties: Camp Hosts; Facilities Maintenance; Grounds maintenance

Times Volunteers Needed Most: late spring to early fall

Little Talbot Island State Park - District 2

Brian Stinson, Park Ranger/Volunteer Coordinator

12157 Heckscher Dr.

Jacksonville, FL 32226

(904) 251-2324

Brian.Stinson@dep.state.fl.us

http://www.floridastateparks.org/littletalbotisland/default.cfm

No. of Campground Hosts: 2

Campsite Amenities: Water/Electric and a Dump station

Electrical Types: 30Amps

RV/Trailer Rig Length Limit: 30'

No. of Residential/Park Hosts: 3

Campsite Amenities: Water/Electric/Sewer

Electrical Types: 30Amps

RV/Trailer Rig Length Limit: 40'

FREE Extras: None

Other Park Amenities/Notes: None

Hours Required: 20 Hours per week

Length of Stay: 2 to 4 months

Examples of Duties: Camp Hosts, Maintenance, Grounds keeping, Ranger Station, Toll Collection, Office Assistant, Mechanic

Times Volunteers Needed Most: Summer months sometimes

Long Key State Park - District 5

Richard "RJ" Simpson, Park Services Specialist/Volunteer Coordinator

P.O. Box 776

Long Key, FL 33001

(305) 664-4815

rj.simpson@dep.state.fl.us

http://www.floridastateparks.org/longkey/default.cfm

No. of Campground Hosts: 2

Campsite Amenities: Water/Electric and a dump station

Electrical Type: 50Amp

RV/Trailer Rig Length Limits: 1 at 31', 1 at 45' and 2 at 40'

No. of Residential Hosts: 2

Campsite Amenities: both located in the campground behind bathhouse

FREE Extras: Laundry

Other Park Amenities/Notes: None

Hours Required: 20 Hours per week per person

Length of Stay: 2 to 4 months

Examples of Duties: Camp Hosts, trail maintenance, facility repairs or upgrades, and equipment maintenance

Times Volunteers Needed Most: None really they are booked over a year in advance

Lovers Key State Park - District 4

Catherine E Moses, Park Services Specialist/Volunteer Coordinator

8700 Estero Blvd

Ft. Myers Beach, FL 33931

(239) 463-4588

catherine.moses@dep.state.fl.us

http://www.floridastateparks.org/loverskey/default.cfm

No. of Campground Hosts: 0

No. of Residential/Park Hosts: 6

Campsite Amenities: Water/Electric/Sewer

Electrical Type: 50Amp

RV/Trailer Rig Length Limit: None

FREE Extras: Ice Machine and access to shower at shop

Other Park Amenities/Notes: asks for $10/month for Washer/Dryer Maintenance, Concession Discount on Bikes, Canoes, Kayaks

Hours Required: 32 Hours a week per site

Length of Stay: 2 to 4 months

Examples of Duties: Facilities Maintenance; Tram Driver; Grounds Maintenance; Special Projects and Events Helpers

Times Volunteers Needed Most: Sometimes during the summer months

Lower Wekiva River Preserve State Park- District 3

Scott E Mowry, Park Services Specialist-Volunteer Coordinator

1800 Wekiwa Cir

Apopka, FL 32712

(407) 884-2006

scott.mowry@dep.state.fl.us

http://www.floridastateparks.org/lowerwekivariver/default.cfm

No. of Campground Hosts: 2

Campsite Amenities: Water/Electric/Sewer

Electrical Type: 30AMPs

RV/Trailer Rig Length Limit: None

No. of Residential/Park Hosts: 0

FREE Extras: None

Other Park Amenities/Notes: None

Hours Required: 20 Hours per Week

Length of Stay: 2 to 4 months

Examples of Duties: Campground Maintenance, Facilities Cleaning and Maintenance, Grounds Maintenance

Times Volunteers Needed Most: Summer months

Madison Blue Spring State Park - District 2

Margaret H Polino, Park Services Specialist/Volunteer Coordinator

8300 N.E. State Road 6

Lee, FL 32059

(850) 971-5003

margaret.polino@dep.state.fl.us

http://www.floridastateparks.org/madisonbluespring/default.cfm

No. of Campground Hosts: 0

No. of Residential Hosts: 3

Campsite Amenities: Water/Electric with central holding tank

Electrical Types: 30Amp

RV/Trailer Rig Length Limits: None

FREE Extras: None

Other Park Amenities/Notes: Little to no cellphone reception within the park

Hours Required: 20 hours per week

Length of Stay: 2 to 4 months

Examples of Duties: Bathroom cleaning, grounds-keeping, special projects, office help and ranger station

Times Volunteers Most Needed: April to September

Marjorie Ross Carr Cross Florida Greenways - District 3

Bre Ximines, Park Services Specialist/Volunteer Coordinator

8282 SE HWY 314

Ocala, FL 34470

(352) 236-7143

bre.ximenes@dep.state.fl.us

http://www.floridastateparks.org/crossflorida/default.cfm

No. of Campground Hosts: 8

Campsite Amenities: Water/Electric/Sewer

Electrical Types: 30/50Amp

RV/Trailer Rig Length Limits: None

No. of Residential Hosts: 0

FREE Extras: None

Other Park Amenities/Notes: Rodman and Shangri-La have coin Laundries;

Hours Required: 20 Hours per Week

Length of Stay: 2 to 4 months

Example of Duties: Campground Host Duties, Ranger Station Duties and Special Projects

Times Volunteers Needed Most: None mostly booked in all parks a year or more in advanced.

Campground Locations

Rodman Campground

410 Rodman Dam Rd

Palatka, FL 32177 386326-2846

Ross Prairie Campground

10660 SW Hwy 200

Dunnellon, FL 34431 352732-2606

Santos Campground

3080 SE 80th St

Ocala, FL 34491 352369-2693

Shangri La Campground

12788 SW 69 Ct

Ocala, FL 34471 352347-1163

Manatee Springs State Park - District 2

Teri L. Graves, Park Service Specialist/Volunteer Coordinator

11650 NW 115th St

Chiefland, FL 32626

(352) 493-6072

teri.l.graves@dep.state.fl.us

http://www.floridastateparks.org/manateesprings/default.cfm

No. of Campground Hosts: 3

Campsite Amenities: Water/Electric with a Dump Station and 1 site with Sewer

Electric Type: 30Amp

RV/Trailer Rig Length Limit: 40'

Tent Camping: Possible contact Coordinator directly

No. of Residential/Park Hosts: 4

Campsite Amenities: Water/Electric/Sewer

Electrical Type: 30Amp

RV/Trailer Rig Length Limit: 40'

FREE Extras: Laundry; Firewood; Ice

Other Park Amenities/Notes: The 1st 40 Campsites are being renovated over the next 12 months beginning August 2014

Hours Required: 20 hours per week

Length of Stay: 2 to 4 months

Examples of Duties: Regular Campground Host Duties, Ranger Station Volunteers, and Waterfront volunteers

Times Volunteers Needed Most: late spring to early fall

Marjorie Kinnan Rawlings Historic State Park - District 2

Valerie Rivers, Park Manager/Volunteer Coordinator

18700 S. County Road 325

Cross Creek, FL 32640

(352) 466-3672

valerie.rivers@dep.state.fl.us

http://www.floridastateparks.org/marjoriekinnanrawlings/default.cfm

No. of Campground Hosts: 0

No. of Residential/Park Hosts: 2

Campsite Amenities: Water/Electric/Sewer

Electrical Types: 30/50AMPs

RV/Trailer Length Limit: 40'

FREE Extras: laundry

Other Park Amenities/Notes: use of the park after closing

Hours Required: 20 hours per week

Length of Stay: 2 to 4 months

Examples of Duties: Assist the staff directly with visitor services, tours, maintenance, and special projects.

Times Volunteers Needed Most: Late spring to early fall

Mike Roess Gold Head Branch State Park - District 2

Steven Earl, Park Ranger/Volunteer Coordinator

6239 State Road 21

Keystone Heights, FL 32656

(352) 473-4701

Steven.Earl@dep.state.fl.us

http://www.floridastateparks.org/mikeroess/default.cfm

No. of Campground Hosts: 3

Campsite Amenities: Water/Electric with a Dump station

Electrical Types: (2) with 20/30 and (1) 20/30/50

RV/Trailer Rig Length Limit: 45'

Tent Camping: Might be possible Check with Volunteer Coordinator

No. of Residential Hosts: 8

Campsite Amenities: Water/Electric/Sewer

Electrical Types: 20/30/50Amps

RV/Trailer Rig Length Limit: 45'

FREE Extras: Laundry, Ice, Firewood

Other Park Amenities/Notes: Canoe Usage and Recreation Facility for Potluck

Hours Required: 20 hours per week

Length of Stay: 2 to 4 months

Examples of Duties: Maintenance, Campground Host weekdays, Campground Host weekends, Park Clean-Up weekdays, Park Clean-Up weekends, Cabin Operations Assistant, Resource Management, Volunteer Coordinator Assistant, and Special Projects

Times Volunteers Needed Most: Summer Months

Myakka River State Park - District 4

Teresa Good, Park Service Specialist/Volunteer Coordinator

13208 State Road 72

Sarasota, FL 34241

(941) 373-7839

teresa.good@dep.state.fl.us

http://www.floridastateparks.org/myakkariver/default.cfm

No. of Campground Hosts: 4 Non-Peak; 6 during the high season

Campsite Amenities: Water/Electric/Sewer

Electric Types: 15/30/50Amps

RV/Trailer Rig Length Limit: 31' in two of the campgrounds and up to 40' in newer one

Tent Camping: May be Possible Check with Volunteer Coordinator

No. of Residential/Park Hosts: up to 16 during the high season

Campsite Amenities: Water/Electric/Sewer

Electrical Types: 15/30/50Amps

RV/Trailer Rig Length Limit: 35'

FREE Extras: Ice

Other Park Amenities/Notes: Reduced Price Coin Laundry

Hours Required: 20 hours per week

Length of Stay: 2 to 4 months

Example of Duties: Camp Hosts Duties; Facilities Maintenance; Grounds Maintenance; Event Helpers; Ranger Station;

Times Volunteers Needed Most: Late spring into early fall

Nature Coast Trails- District 2

Anthony (Kirk) Marhefka, Park Services Specialist/Volunteer Coordinator

18020 N.W. Hwy 19

Fanning Springs, FL 32693

(352) 535-5181

Kirk.Marhefka@dep.state.fl.us

http://www.floridastateparks.org/naturecoast/default.cfm

No. of Campground Hosts: 0

No. of Residential Hosts: 1

Campsite Amenities: Water/Electric/Sewer

Electric Types: 30/50Amps

RV/Trailer Rig Length Limit: 40'

FREE Extras: None

Other Park Amenities/Notes: None

Hours Required: 20 hours per week

Length of Stay: 2 to 4 months

Examples of Duties: Trail Maintenance; facilities maintenance; customer service

Times Volunteers Needed Most: Summer Months

Ochlockonee River State Park - District 1

Jason Vickery, Park Services Specialist/Volunteer Coordinator

P. O. Box 5

Sopchoppy, FL 32358

(850) 962-2771

Jason.Vickery@dep.state.fl.us

http://www.floridastateparks.org/ochlockoneeriver/default.cfm

No. of Campground Hosts: 1

Campsite Amenities: Water/Electric/Sewer

Electrical Types: 30/50Amp

RV/Trailer Rig Length Limit: 35'

No. of Residential/Park Hosts: 0

FREE Extras: Laundry

Other Park Amenities/Hours: None

Hours Required: 20 hours per week

Length of Stay: 2 to 4 months

Examples of Duties: volunteers to help close the park, maintain our day use areas, address maintenance needs, provide great customer service to our visitors

Times Volunteers Needed Most: Summertime

O'Leno State Park - District 2

Cynthia Preston, Park Services Specialist/Volunteer Coordinator

410 S.E. O'Leno Park Rd

High Springs, FL 32643

(386) 454-4201

Cynthia.F.Preston@dep.state.fl.us

http://www.floridastateparks.org/oleno/default.cfm

No. of Campground Hosts: 2

Campsite Amenities: Water/Electric/Sewer

Electrical Types: 30/50Amps

RV/Trailer Rig Length Limit: 45'

No. of Residential/Park Hosts: 2

Campsite Amenities: Water/Electric and a dump station

Electrical Type: 30Amps

RV/Trailer Rig Length Limits: 45'

FREE Extras: None

Other Park Amenities/Notes: Laundry - ask for $20 donation to go towards care of machines

Hours Required: 20 hours per week

Length of Stay: 2 to 4 months

Examples of Duties: Campground Hosts; Field Volunteers; Facilities and Grounds Maintenance

Times Volunteers Needed the Most: Summertime

Oleta River State Park - District 5

Jennifer E Roberts, Park Services Specialist/Volunteer Coordinator

3400 N.E. 163rd St.

North Miami, FL 33160

(305) 919-1844

jennifer.e.roberts@dep.state.fl.us

http://www.floridastateparks.org/oletariver/default.cfm

No. of Campground Hosts: 1 (Cabin Cleaners)

Campsite Amenities: Water/Electric/Sewer

Electrical Types: 30/50Amp

RV/Trailer Rig Length Limit: None - Located Behind the Cabins

No. of Residential/Park Hosts: 3

Campsite Amenities: Water/Electric/Sewer

Electrical Types: 30/50Amp

RV/Trailer Rig Length Limit: None

FREE Extras: Laundry

Other Park Amenities/Notes: none

Hours Required: 20 hours per week

Length of Stay: 2 to 4 months

Examples of Duties: Cabin Cleaners, maintenance positions that assist with working in our ranger station, general park maintenance and driving our seven passenger golf cart to assist visitors on the weekends.

Times Volunteers Needed Most: Summer Months

Orman House Historic State Park - District 1

Michael Kinnett, Park Services Specialist/Volunteer Coordinator

177 5th St.

Apalachicola, FL 32320

(850) 927-2111

Michael.Kinnett@dep.state.fl.us

http://www.floridastateparks.org/ormanhouse/default.cfm

No. of Campground Hosts: 0

No. of Residential/Park Hosts: 2

Campsite Amenities: Water/Electric/Sewer

Electrical Types: 50Amps

RV/Trailer Rig Length Limit: None

FREE Extras: None

Other Park Amenities/Notes: Fenced in area for Volunteers to let their pets run

Hours Required: 20 hours per week

Length of Stay: 2 to 4 months but could stay as much as 8 months from March to October as you are in between fiscal years,

Examples of Duties: Gardening, Landscaping, Tour Guides, Cleaning an Antebellum Mansion

Times Volunteers Needed Most: May to October

Oscar Scherer State Park - District 4

Cristy M Disbrow, Park Services Coordinator/Volunteer Coordinator

1843 South Tamiami Trail

Osprey, FL 34229

(941) 483-5956

cristy.disbrow@dep.state.fl.us

http://www.floridastateparks.org/oscarscherer/default.cfm

No. of Campground Hosts: 4

Campsite Amenities: Water/Electric and a Dump Station

Electrical Types: 20/30Amp

RV/Trailer Rig Length Limit: 36'

No. of Residential/Park Hosts: 6

Campsite Amenities: Water/Electric and a Dump Station (2 of the 6 has sewers onsite and the remaining 4 will have within next 2 years)

Electrical Types: 20/30Amp working on adding 50Amp throughout the Park

RV/Trailer Rig Length Limit: 36'

FREE Extras: Laundry and Free Firewood

Other Park Amenities/Notes: 50% Pancake Breakfast

Hours Required: 20 per week for Singles; 32 per week for Couples

Length of Stay: 2 to 4 months

Examples of Duties: Camp Host; shop maintenance, general maintenance, administration (clerical), toll collector, Nature Center staff, program coordinators and event support

Times Volunteers Needed Most: May through November, with July, August and September (the quiet and "warm" months) are the hardest to get volunteers

Paynes Creek Historic State Park - District 4

Christy Lanier, OPS Administrative Assistant/Volunteer Coordinator

888 Lake Branch Rd

Bowling Green, FL 33834

(863) 375-4717

christy.lanier@dep.state.fl.us

http://www.floridastateparks.org/paynescreek/default.cfm

No. of Campground Hosts: 0

No. of Residential/Park Hosts: 7

Campsite Amenities: Water/Electric/Sewer

Electrical Types: 30/50Amp

RV/Trailer Rig Length Limit: None

FREE Extras: Washer/Dryer, Lounge, Refrigerator, Shower

Other Park Amenities/Notes: None

Hours Required: 20 per week

Length of Stay: 2 to 4 and up to 5 months for special projects

Examples of Duties: cleaning restrooms, garbage collecting, trail maintenance, painting, plumbing, mowing, assisting with special events, visitor Services, ranger station, assisting Ranger in other projects

Times Volunteers Needed Most: summer months

Paynes Prairie Preserve State Park - District 2

Amber Roux, Park Services Specialist/Volunteer Coordinator

100 Savannah Blvd

Micanopy, FL 32667

(352) 466-4966

Amber.Roux@dep.state.fl.us

http://www.floridastateparks.org/paynesprairie/default.cfm

No. of Campground Hosts: 2

Campsite Amenities: Water/Electric/Sewer

Electrical Types: 30/50Amps

RV/Trailer Rig Length Limit: 50'

No. of Residential/Park Hosts:

Campsite Amenities: Water/Electric/Sewer

Electrical Types: 30/50Amps

RV/Trailer Rig Length Limit: 50'

FREE Extras: Laundry

Other Park Amenities/Notes: None

Hours Required: 20 hours per week

Length of Stay Limits: 2 to 4 months

Examples of Duties: Campground Host duties, helping in ranger station, special projects and events

Times Year Volunteers Needed Most: Summer

Ponce de Leon Springs State Park - District 1

Scott A Sweeney, Park Services Specialist/Volunteer Coordinator

2860 Ponce de Leon Springs Rd

Ponce de Leon, FL 32455

(850) 638-6130

scott.sweeney@dep.state.fl.us

http://www.floridastateparks.org/poncedeleonsprings/default.cfm

No. of Campground Hosts: 0

No. of Residential/Park Host: 2

Campsite Amenities: Water/Electric/Sewer

Electrical Types: 30/50Amp

RV/Trailer Rig Length Limit: 45'

FREE Extras: Laundry, Ice, Firewood

Other Park Amenities/Notes: None

Hours Required: 20 to 24 hours per week

Length of Stay: 2 to 4 months

Examples of Duties: Ranger Station, cleaning of facilities, mowing, different maintenance jobs requiring carpentry, plumbing, painting and landscaping skills.

Times Volunteers Needed Most: Summer

Rainbow Springs State Park- District 2

Monay L Markey, Park Services Specialist/Volunteer Coordinator

19158 SW 81st Place Rd

Dunnellon, FL 34432

(352) 465-8520

monay.markey@dep.state.fl.us

http://www.floridastateparks.org/rainbowsprings/default.cfm

No. of Campground Hosts: 2

Campsite Amenities: Water/Electric/Sewer

Electrical Types: 20/30/50Amps

RV/Trailer Rig Length Limits: none

No. of Residential/Park Hosts: 4

Campsite Amenities: Water/Electric/Sewer

Electrical Types: 20/30/50AMPs

FREE Extras: none

Other Park Amenities/Notes: coin laundry in campground

Hours Required: 24 Hours per week

Length of Stay: 2 to 4 months

Examples of Duties: Campground Hosts Duties, Maintenance Host Duties, Cleaning the springs area, mowing, etc.

Times Volunteers Most Needed: Summer

Ravine Gardens State Park - District 3

Lauren A Watkins, Park Services Specialist/Volunteer Coordinator

1600 Twigg St.

Palatka, FL 32177

(386) 329-3721

lauren.watkins@dep.state.fl.us

http://www.floridastateparks.org/ravinegardens/default.cfm

No. of Campground Hosts: 0

No. of Residential/Park Hosts: 2

Campsite Amenities: Water/Electric/Sewer

Electrical Types: 20/30/50AMPs

RV/Trailer Rig Length Limits: 38'

FREE Extras: Free Ice

Other Park Amenities/Notes: none

Hours Required: 25 Hours per week

Length of Stay: 1 to 4 months, More time may be given it depends on Needs of the Park

Examples of Duties: Primarily gardening and landscaping, as well as helping with some special events.

Times Volunteers Needed Most: Late spring to early fall

River Rise Preserve State Park - District 2

Cynthia Preston, Park Services Specialist/Volunteer Coordinator

410 S.E. O'Leno Park Rd.

High Springs, FL 32643

(386) 454-4201

Cynthia.F.Preston@dep.state.fl.us

http://www.floridastateparks.org/riverrise/default.cfm

No. of Campground Hosts: 1

Campsite Amenities: Water/Electric/Sewer

Electrical Types: 30AMPS

RV/Trailer Rig Length Limit: 40'

No. of Residential Hosts: 0

FREE Extras: None

Other Park Amenities/Notes: None

Hours Required: 20 hours per week

Length of Stay: 2 to 4 months

Examples of Duties: Equestrian Campground Host, Facilities Maintenance; Grounds Maintenance

Times Volunteers Needed Most: Summer Months

Rock Springs Run State Reserve - District 3

Scott E Mowry, Park Services Specialist/Volunteer Coordinator

1800 Wekiwa Cir.

Apopka, FL 32712

(407) 884-2006

scott.mowry@dep.state.fl.us

http://www.floridastateparks.org/rockspringsrun/default.cfm

No. Of Campground Hosts: 1

Campsite Amenities: Water/Electric/Sewer

Electrical Types: 30AMP

RV/Trailer Rig Length Limit: None

No. of Residential Hosts: 0

FREE Extras: None

Other Park Amenities/Notes: None

Hours Required: 20 Hours per week

Length of Stay: 2 to 4 months

Examples of Duties: Campground hosting duties

Times Volunteers Needed Most: Summer months

San Felasco Hammock Preserve State Park - District 2

Randall E Brown, Resident Park Manager II/Volunteer Coordinator

12720 NW 109 Ln.

Alachua, FL 32615

(386) 462-7905

randall.e.brown@dep.state.fl.us

http://www.floridastateparks.org/sanfelascohammock/default.cfm

No. of Campground Hosts: 0

No. of Residential Hosts: 3

Campsite Amenities: Water/Electric/Sewer

Electrical Types: 30/50AMPS

RV/Trailer Rig Length Limit: 40'

FREE Extras: laundry

Other Park Amenities/Notes: None

Hours Required: 20 hours per week

Length of Stay: 2 to 4 months

Examples of Duties: Maintaining Trails, General Maintenance of Buildings and Facilities, Grounds Maintenance, Helping Rangers with park Horses Care and Feeding

Times Volunteers Needed Most: Summer

San Marcos de Apalache Historic State Park - District 1

Theresa C Messler (Terri), Park Services Specialist/Volunteer Coordinator

148 Old Fort Rd.

St. Marks, FL 32355

(850) 922-6007

Terri.Messler@dep.state.fl.us

http://www.floridastateparks.org/sanmarcos/default.cfm

No. of Campground Hosts: 0

No. of Residential Hosts: call park for more information

Campsite Amenities: Water/Electric/Sewer

Electrical Types: 50Amp

RV/Trailer Rig Length Limits: none

FREE Extras: none

Other Park Amenities/Notes: Great fishing, nearby boat ramp, good TV, satellite and cell service.

Hours Required: 20 hours minimum per week, more may be required

Length of Stay: 2 to 4 months

Examples of Duties: call park for more information

Times Volunteers Needed Most: volunteers always needed during summer months

Savannas Preserve State Park - District 5

Elizabeth "Wren" Underwood, Park Services Specialist/Volunteer Coordinator

2541 Walton Rd.

Port St. Lucie, FL 34952

(772) 340-7530

Elizabeth.Underwood@dep.state.fl.us

http://www.floridastateparks.org/savannas/default.cfm

No. of Campground Hosts: 0

No. of Residential/Park hosts: 4

Campsite Amenities: Water/Electric/Sewer

Electrical Types: 1 is 30Amp; 3 are 50Amp

RV/Trailer Rig Length Limit: 40'

FREE Extras: None

Other Park Amenities/Notes: None

Hours Required: 20 hours per week

Length of Stays: 2 to 4 months

Examples of Duties: education center docent and administrative support, grounds and fleet maintenance,

Times Volunteers Needed Most: Summer Time

Sebastian Inlet State Park - District 3

Michael Moreno, Park Ranger/Volunteer Coordinator

9700 South State Road A1A

Melbourne Beach, FL 32951

(321) 984-4852

michael.moreno@dep.state.fl.us

http://www.floridastateparks.org/sebastianinlet/default.cfm

No. of Campground Hosts: 2

Campsite Amenities: Water/Electric/Sewer

Electrical Types: 20/30/50AMPs

RV/Trailer Rig Length Limit: 32'

No. of Residential/Park Hosts: 6

Campsite Amenities: Water/Electric/Sewer

Electrical Types: 20/30/50AMPS

RV/Trailer Rig Length Limit: 32'

FREE Extras: Washer/Dryer

Other Park Amenities/Notes: Discount at Concession

Hours Required: 20 Hours Single/40Hours Couples

Length of Stay: 2 to 4 months

Examples of Duties: Campground Host, Maintenance Duties, Museum Attendants

Times Volunteers Needed Most: Sometimes during the summer

Silver Springs State Park - District 3

Stacey Lamborn, Park Services Specialist/Volunteer Coordinator

1425 N.E. 58th Ave.

Ocala, FL 34470

(352) 236-7148

stacey.lamborn@dep.state.fl.us

http://www.floridastateparks.org/silversprings/default.cfm

No. of Campground Host: 4

Campsite Amenities: Water/Electric, Sewers coming

Electrical Types: 30/50AMPS

RV/Trailer Rig Length Limit: 40'

No. of Residential/Park Hosts: 1

Campsite Amenities: Water/Electric, Sewers coming

Electrical Types: 30/50AMPS

RV/Trailer Rig Length Limit: 40'

FREE Extras: None

Other Park Amenities/Notes: coin laundry in campground

Hours Required: 20 Hours per week

Length of Stay: 2 to 4 months

Examples of Duties: toll booth operator, ranger station assistant, museum docent, Education Center guide, administration assistant, interpretive and educational programs, Park Watch/River Patrol, general gardening, general maintenance, campground host

Times Volunteers Needed Most: Summer

St. Andrews State Park - District 1

Melissa Shoemaker, Park Services Specialist/Volunteer Coordinator

4607 State Park Ln.

Panama City, FL 32408

(850) 233-5141

Melissa.LeMatty@dep.state.fl.us

http://www.floridastateparks.org/standrews/default.cfm

No. of Campground Hosts: 6

Campsite Amenities: Water/Electric and a Dump Station

Electrical Types: Mixture of 30 and 50 Amp

RV/Trailer Rig Length Limit: 40'

No. of Residential/Park Hosts: 8

Campsite Amenities: Water/Electric - 3 sites have sewers

Electric Types: Mixture of 30 and 50 Amp

RV/Trailer Rig Length Limit: 40'

FREE Extras: Washer/Dryer and Ice machine

Other Park Amenities/Notes: None

Hours Required: 20 hours per week

Length of Stay: 2 to 4 months

Examples of Duties: Campground Hosts, Maintenance, Grounds, Ranger Station

Times Volunteers Needed Most: Mostly Summers

St. Sebastian River Preserve State Park - District 3

Kenneth B Temple, Park Services Specialist/Volunteer Coordinator

1000 Buffer Preserve Dr.

Fellsmere, FL 32948

(321) 953-5004

kenneth.temple@dep.state.fl.us

http://www.floridastateparks.org/stsebastianriver/default.cfm

No. of Campground Hosts: 2

Campsite Amenities: Water/Electric/Sewer

Electrical Types: 30/50AMPs

RV/Trailer Rig Limits: None

No. of Residential Hosts: 5

Campsite Amenities: Water/Electric/Sewer

Electrical Types: 30/50AMPS

RV/Trailer Rig Length Limit: None

FREE Extras: Laundry and Ice

Other Park Amenities/Notes: None

Examples of Duties: Clean and Man Visitors Center, Open and Close Gates, Check in Campers, Clean Grounds, Man Ranger Station

Times Volunteers Needed Most: April through October

Stephen Foster Folk Culture Center State Park - District 2

Stephanie L McClain, Park Services Specialist/Volunteer Coordinator

P.O. Box G

White Springs, FL 32096

(386) 397-4461

stephanie.mcclain@dep.state.fl.us

http://www.floridastateparks.org/stephenfoster/default.cfm

No. of Campground Hosts: 2

Campsite Amenities: Water/Electric and a Dump Station

Electrical Types: 30/50Amp

RV/Trailer Rig Length Limit: 50'

No. of Residential/Park Hosts: 7

Campsite Amenities: Water/Electric - Sewers on 3 Craft Volunteer Sites Working on 4 More

Electrical Types: 30/50Amp

RV/Trailer Rig Length Limits: 50'

FREE Extras: Free Laundry; Ice; Firewood, Gift Shop has Free Water/Coffee/Lemonade for Volunteers

Other Park Amenities/Notes: Has double the volunteers spaces during the peak season

Hours Required: 20 hours per week

Length of Stay: 2 to 4 months

Examples of Duties: Campground Hosts, Craft Village Instructors, Grounds Maintenance, Facilities Maintenance, Museum Docent

Times Volunteers Needed Most: Late Spring to Early Fall

Suwannee River State Park - District 2

Rianna Elliott, Park Ranger/Volunteer Coordinator

3631 201st Path

Live Oak, FL 32060

(386) 294-3667

Rianna.Elliott@dep.state.fl.us

http://www.floridastateparks.org/suwanneeriver/default.cfm

No. of Campground Hosts: 2

Campsite Amenities: Water/Electric/Sewer

Electrical Types: 20/30/50Amp

RV/Trailer Rig Length Limits: none

No. of Residential Hosts: 4

Campsite Amenities: Water/Electric/Sewer

Electrical Types: 20/30/50Amp

RV/Trailer Rig Length Limits: none

FREE Extras: Washer/Dryer/Firewood

Other Park Amenities/Notes: none

Hours Required: 20 hours per week minimum, more may be required

Length of Stay: 2 to 4 months

Examples of Duties: Campground Host duties, ranger station assistance, assist the park ranger with programs and grounds, special projects

Times Volunteers Most Needed: late spring to early fall

Suwannee River Wilderness Trail - District 2

Larry W. Arrant, Park Services Specialist/Volunteer Coordinator

4298 NW CR 292

Mayo, FL 32066

(386) 294-3667

larry.arrant@dep.state.fl.us

http://www.floridastateparks.org/wilderness/default.cfm

No. of Campground Hosts: 5

Campsite Amenities: Water/Electric/Sewer

Electrical Types: 20/30/50Amps

RV/Trailer Rig Length Limits: 40'

No. of Residential/Park Hosts: 0

FREE Extras: Laundry/Firewood

Other Park Amenities/Notes: Some sites have extra storage and use of extra Refrigerator/Freezer - Woods Ferry, Holton Creek, Dowling Park, Peacock Slough and Adams Tract River Camps

Hours Required: 20 hours per week

Length of Stay: 2 to 4 months

Examples of Duties: Campground Hosts Duties; Grounds Maintenance; Keep Count of Visitors and Campers for Monthly Report; Monitoring Chlorine Levels in water well; Selling Firewood and sometimes Ice; In charge of the river camps without rangers present; Greet all visitors and campers

Times Volunteers Needed Most: Late spring to early fall

TH Stone Memorial St Joseph's Peninsula State Park - District 1

Danny Kemp, Resident Assistant Park Manager/Volunteer Coordinator

8899 Cape San Blas Rd

Port St. Joe, FL 32456

(850) 227-1327

danny.kemp@dep.state.fl.us

http://www.floridastateparks.org/stjoseph/default.cfm

No. of Campground Hosts: 4

Campsite Amenities: Water/Electric and Dump a Station

Electrical Type: 30Amp

RV/Trailer Rig Length Limits: 40' (Some sites are not very wide)

Tent Camping: None

No. of Residential/Park Hosts: 2

Campsite Amenities: Water/Electric/Sewer

Electrical Types: 30Amp

RV/Trailer Rig Limits: 40'

FREE Extras: Laundry/Ice Machine at the Shop

Other Park Amenities/Notes: Concession Store and food and Free Wi-Fi. The cellphone service is not very good in the camping and cabin areas.

Hours Required: 20 hours per person per week - Good volunteers will do more

Length of Stay: 1 to 4 months (Normally 3 Months)

Examples of Duties: Campground Hosts; Facilities Maintenance; Grounds-keeping; Special Projects

Times Volunteers Needed Most: Sometimes During Summer Months

Three Rivers State Park - District 1

Wesley A. Jones, Park Ranger /Volunteer Coordinator

7908 Three Rivers Park Rd.

Sneads, FL 32460

(850) 482-9006

wesley.jones@dep.state.fl.us

http://www.floridastateparks.org/threerivers/default.cfm

No. of Campground Hosts: 2

Campsite Amenities: Water/Electric/Sewer

Electrical Types: 30/50Amp

RV/Trailer Rig Length Limits: None

No. of Residential Hosts: 2

Campsite Amenities: Water/Electric/Sewer

Electrical Types: 30/50Amp

RV/Trailer Rig Length Limits: None

FREE Extras: Laundry and Firewood

Other Park Amenities/Notes: None

Hours Required: 20 hours per week

Length of Stay: 2 to 4 months

Examples of Duties: Campground Host duties, assisting park rangers with their duties

Times Volunteers Most Needed: January to April

Tomoka State Park - District 3

Agnes S Armstrong, Park Services Specialist/Volunteer Coordinator

2099 North Beach St.

Ormond Beach, FL 32174

(386) 676-4050

aggie.armstrong@dep.state.fl.us

http://www.floridastateparks.org/tomoka/default.cfm

No. of Campground Hosts: 4 during peak season (Oct to April)

Campsite Amenities: Water/Electric and a Dump Station

Electrical Types: 30/50AMPs

RV/Trailer Rig Length Limit: 34'

No. of Residential/Park Hosts: 2

Campsite Amenities: Water/Electric/Sewer

Electrical Types: 30/50AMPS

RV/Trailer Rig Length Limit: 34'

FREE Extras: none

Other Park Amenities/Notes: Coin Laundry in one of the Campgrounds

Hours Required: 20 hours per week per campsite

Length of Stay: 2 to 4 months

Examples of Duties: Campground Hosts, Facilities and Equipment Maintenance, Grounds-keeping, Cleaning Bathrooms, Carpentry, Mechanic, Special Park Projects

Times Volunteers Needed Most: Summer Months

Topsail Hill Preserve State Park - District 1

Wilbur "Fred" Provost, Park Services Specialist/Volunteer Coordinator

7525 W. Scenic Highway 30A

Santa Rosa Beach, FL 32459

(850) 267-8330

wilbur.provost@dep.state.fl.us

http://www.floridastateparks.org/topsailhill/default.cfm

No. of Campground Hosts: 6

Campsite Amenities: Water/Electric/Sewer

Electrical Types: 50Amp

RV/Trailer Rig Length Limits: 36' to 45'

No. of Residential/Park Hosts: 11 during Peak Season

Campsite Amenities: Water/Electric/Sewer

Electrical Types: 50Amp

RV/Trailer Rig Length Limit: 45'

FREE Extras: Laundry and Free Cable

Other Park Amenities/Notes: Store Discounts; pool; shuffleboard

Hours Required: 30 hours per week

Length of Stay: 2 to 4 months

Examples of Duties: Mar. to Oct. those volunteers in the campground run, stock and clean the camp store; housekeeping includes cleaning camp bathrooms and cabins; and tram operators take people to and from the beach/canoe area and they keep track of empty campsites. Nov. to Feb. number of housekeeping positions reduced sites are for maintenance volunteers that keep the facilities and equipment in working order.

Times Volunteers Needed Most: none, occasional summer months

Torreya State Park - District 1

Robert Y Crombie, Park Ranger/Volunteer Coordinator

2576 N.W. Torreya Park Rd.

Bristol, FL 32321

(850) 643-2674

Robert.Crombie@dep.state.fl.us

http://www.floridastateparks.org/torreya/default.cfm

No. of Campground Hosts: 1

Campsite Amenities: Water/Electric/Sewer

Electrical Types: 20/30/50Amp

RV/Trailer Rig Length Limit: 40'

No. of Residential Hosts: 0

FREE Extras: laundry

Other Park Amenities/Notes: None

Hours Required: 20 hours per week

Length of Stay: 2 to 4 months

Examples of Duties: Campground Hosts Duties, Customer Service, Minor Maintenance, Painting, Cleaning of Historic Gregory House, Day Use Area Cleaning

Times Volunteers Needed Most: Summer Months

Troy Springs State Park - District 2

Tina Miller, Park Services Specialist/Volunteer Coordinator

674 N.E. Troy Springs Rd.

Branford, FL 32008

(386) 935-4835

tina.miller@dep.state.fl.us

http://www.floridastateparks.org/troyspring/default.cfm

No. of Campground Hosts: 0

No. of Residential/Park Hosts: 2

Campsite Amenities: Water/Electric/Sewer

Electrical Types: 20/30/50Amps

RV/Trailer Rig Length Limit: 40'

FREE Extras: None

Other Park Amenities/Notes: None

Hours Required: 20 hours per week

Length of Stay: 2 to 4 months

Examples of Duties: Facilities Maintenance; Opening and Closing Park; Grounds Maintenance; Greeting Visitors and helping Park Rangers

Times Volunteers Needed Most: Late spring to early fall and sometimes winter

Washington Oaks Gardens State Park - District 3

Aleta R Paolini (Renee), Resident Park Manager II/Volunteer Coordinator

6400 North Oceanshore Blvd

Palm Coast, FL 32137

(386) 446-6780

renee.paolini@dep.state.fl.us

http://www.floridastateparks.org/washingtonoaks/default.cfm

No. of Campground Hosts: 0

No. of Residential/Park Hosts: 2

Campsite Amenities: Water/Electric/Sewer

Electrical Types: 30/50AMPs

RV/Trailer Rig Length Limit: None

FREE Extras: None

Other Park Amenities/Notes: Contact park for more information.

Hours Required: 20 Hours per week

Length of Stay: 2 to 4 months

Examples of Duties: maintenance, construction, office work, gardening

Times Volunteers Needed Most: Summer

Weeki Wachee Springs State Park - District 4

Toby Brewer, Park Manager/Volunteer Coordinator

6131 Commercial Way

Spring Hill, FL 34606

(352) 592-5656

toby.brewer@dep.state.fl.us

http://www.floridastateparks.org/weekiwachee/default.cfm

No. of Campground Hosts: 0

No. of Residential/Park Hosts: 4

Campsite Amenities: Water/Electric/Sewer

Electrical Types: 30/50Amp

RV/Trailer Rig Length Limit: 40' - has 1 site that is 45'

FREE Extras: Laundry Room

Other Park Amenities/Notes: Plans for additional site in the works

Hours Required: 20 Hours per week

Length of Stay: 2 to 4 months

Examples of Duties: Facilities Maintenance; Grounds Maintenance; Special Projects and Events Helpers

Times Volunteers Needed Most: late spring to early fall

Wekiwa Springs State Park - District 3

Scott E Mowry, Park Services Specialist-Volunteer Coordinator

1800 Wekiwa Cir.

Apopka, FL 32712

(407) 884-2006

scott.mowry@dep.state.fl.us

http://www.floridastateparks.org/wekiwasprings/default.cfm

No. of Campground Hosts: 2

Campsite Amenities: Water/Electric/Sewer

Electrical Types: 30Amps

RV/Trailer Rig Length Limits: None

Tent Camping: Possible Check with Volunteer Coordinator

No. of Residential Hosts: 2

Campsite Amenities: Water/Electric/Sewer

Electrical Types: 30Amps

RV/Trailer Rig Length Limit: None

FREE Extras: None

Other Park Amenities/Notes: None

Hours Required: 20 Hours per Week

Length of Stay: 2 to 4 months

Examples of Duties: Regular Campground Host Duties, grounds maintenance, customer service

Times Volunteers Needed Most: Late spring to early fall

Werner-Boyce Salt Springs State Park - District 4

Michael V. Faustini, Park Ranger/Volunteer Coordinator

PO Box 490

Port Richey, FL 34673

(727) 816-1890

michael.faustini@dep.state.fl.us

http://www.floridastateparks.org/wernerboyce/default.cfm

No. of Campground Hosts: 0

No. of Residential/Park Hosts: 4

Campsite Amenities: Water/Electric/Sewer

Electrical Types: 30Amp

RV/Trailer Rig Length Limit: 40'

FREE Extras: Washer/Dryer, Fridge, Kitchen, Ice Machine

Other Park Amenities/Notes: Boat Ramp, Canoes and Kayaks

Hours Required: 20 hours per week

Length of Stay: 2 to 4 months

Examples of Duties: opening/closing the park, cleaning of visitor areas and shop compound area, lawn maintenance, removal and/or treatment invasive exotic pest plants, carpentry, pluming, administrative work, and mechanical work.

Times Volunteers Needed Most: Summer months

Florida State Parks - Plans for Future Campground/Residential/Parks Hosts Sites

Since we emailed and/or called every single Florida State Park and Trail on the Florida State Park websites for information about "Live On-Site" volunteer campsites we thought we would ask those that do not have any at this time if they plan to have any in the future. Below is a listing of Florida State Parks and Trails that stated they hoped to add them in the future. Since, having live on-site volunteers supplements the park staff, keeps budgets lower and is also a pretty great marketing tool for state parks we hope these and more of them will get the approval and funding for more of these volunteer spaces in the future!

As full-time live on-site volunteers, we also hope that these park planners will take our needs into consideration when getting the approvals and budgets for these campsites. Our simplest needs are a level, stable site with water/electric and SEWERS on-site. There is nothing worse than having to drive over to the dump station every couple of days or emptying your gray and black water tanks into a little blue container and towing it to the dump station. Of course, it is also nice if your RV/Trailer doesn't sink into the ground or tilt over when a storm makes the ground all soggy.

The use of a washer/dryer for free is a great incentive and saves us, the volunteers, so much money and time away from the park. If you provide the little things for your live on-site volunteers they do not have to worry about when and where they can get their clothes clean. Working in a Florida State Park can be a pretty dirty job and RV/Trailers do not have a lot of space for extra clothing. That means you have to wash more times than you would at home.

Of course, if we can have access to a shower with good water pressure and lots of hot water that would so awesome. It can even be located inside a shop building. Women generally need longer showers than men. RV/Trailers generally only have 6 gallons of hot water. And as we get older we all could use a long hot shower to smooth out the aches and pains of working outdoors. These little extras save us propane for our hot water tanks and we don't have to empty our gray water tanks as often.

Finally, the use of an extra refrigerator/freezer is a great savings for volunteers. Since, most of us are on a tight budget with food being among the biggest expenses. It would be great to be able to buy in bulk. Again, trailers and RVs do not have very large spaces to store stuff including in their refrigerators and freezers. Being able to buy extra meat, produce and dairy and have them close by saves us money as well as the time it takes to go into town (wherever they might be located) and grocery shop.

With just a little planning and expense ahead of time you can have more volunteers be interested in coming to your park no matter how big or small or where it is located and even all year long. These little things are what most of us look for when trying to find a place to volunteer.

Bill Baggs Cape Florida State Park - District 5

David Foster, Park Manager

1200 South Crandon Blvd

Key Biscayne, FL 33149

(305) 361-8779

David.Foster@dep.state.fl.us

Overnight boat anchoring, primitive and group camping facilities

HOPES TO ADD 4 SITES THIS COMING YEAR - 2014/2015

Forest Capital Museum State Park - District 2

Debra L Walker, Park Services Specialist/Volunteer Coordinator

204 Forest Park Dr.

Perry, FL 32348

(850) 584-3227

Debra.L.Walker@dep.state.fl.us

Interpretive Exhibit, Visitor Center, Playground, Picnicking, Restrooms and Playground

Does have plans for adding volunteer sites in the future just waiting on funding

Okeechobee Battlefield State Park – District 5

Access to the park from 38th Ave off U.S. Highway 441/98 in Okeechobee County

Acquired on November 30, 2006 and currently managed by Jonathan Dickinson State Park

From the Approved Open Management Plan December 22, 2010

Future Services: Open-air Interpretive Center, Picnic Pavilions, Restrooms, Trails, Reenactment Area,

***Proposed Future Use Plan - Utility hookups should be provided for one or two volunteer hosts sites near the shop area.

To be kept abreast of the current status of the plans please contact:

Mr. Mark Nelson, Park Manager

Jonathan Dickinson State Park

16450 SE Federal Highway

Hobe Sound, Florida 33455

Has no website page on the Florida State Parks Website Yet

Terra Ceia Preserve State Park - District 4

Kevin C Kiser, Resident Park Manager I

130 Terra Ceia Rd

Terra Ceia, FL 34250

(941) 723-4536

kevin.kiser@dep.state.fl.us

Has no web page on the Florida State Parks Website

Currently has boating, canoeing and kayaking, fishing, hiking, historic site, picnicking

Has Plans to add volunteer sites in the future when funding comes through.

FLORIDA COUNTY PARKS

There are 67 counties in the state of Florida and only 32 of those offers camping at county campgrounds. Most, if not all, give special discounts to local residents, do not have an online reservation system and are unable to book in advance as they may be "first-come, first-serve" campgrounds. You may be able to volunteer as a campground host through the county's Parks and Recreation Department. We contacted each of the counties with a county park campground for more information. Below we have listed the counties, the parks name and contact information for the ones that do have volunteers and those that state they will be implementing them in the near future.

You will need to contact each of the campgrounds and/or the county parks and recreation departments to find out more about the application process, requirements and possible future openings. We have listed as many links, contacts, and general information about the county parks as we could gather. Quite a few of them ask that potential volunteers come by the parks and talk to the managers in person. Nearly, all of them will have an application process, background checks, etc.

Even though most will want volunteers to stay for longer lengths of time than with the State parks you just never know what opportunities may arise so keep checking with the county parks of your choice!

Broward County

Broward County Parks and Recreation

950 N.W. 38th St.

Oakland Park, FL 33309

Phone: (954) 357-8100

Fax: (954) 357-5982

parksvolunteers@broward.org

http://www.broward.org/Parks/GetInvolved/Pages/Default.aspx

Bri-Ann Wright, Parks and Recreation Manager III

Easterlin Park

1000 N.W. 38th St.

Oakland Park, FL 33309

Main: (954) 357-5190

Office: (954) 357-5194

Fax: (954) 357-5191

brwright@broward.org

easterlinpark@broward.org

http://www.broward.org/Parks/EasterlinPark/Pages/Default.aspx

Michelle Parks, Parks and Recreation Manager IV

Markham Park

16001 W. State Rd. 84

Sunrise, FL 33326

(954) 357-8868

markhampark@broward.org

http://www.broward.org/Parks/MarkhamPark/Pages/Default.aspx

Derrick Sanders, Parks and Recreation Manager II

Quiet Waters

401 S. Powerline Rd.

Deerfield Beach, FL 33442

Main: (954) 357-5100

Office: (954) 357-5106

Fax: (954) 357-5101

dsanders@broward.org

quietwaterspark@broward.org

http://www.broward.org/Parks/QuietWatersPark/Pages/Default.aspx

*Campground does not have full hookup for RVs

From the Broward County Parks and Recreation Volunteer Program Manual

Description of work involved: Customer service for registered campers within campground area after park closing hours. Duties include, but are not limited to, welcoming campers, assisting with registration and late arrivals, explaining rules and regulations, event/program coordinator, and primary contact for campers' questions and concerns when staff is unavailable. Hosts can assist on monitoring campgrounds and entrance gates on days parks are closed. Hosts may also be asked to assist in the park office; light maintenance within campground sites to include restroom cleaning, grills and fire rings, trash removal, campground inspection prior to and after rentals. Special skills such as carpentry, painting, and grounds keeping will be gratefully accepted.

The park will provide the campground hosts with a designated site determined by park management. Hosts must provide their own camping equipment.

Seeking volunteers who will reside in park's campgrounds for three months, with the opportunity to reapply, pending availability.

Hours volunteers can work: Variable, depending on each park's needs.

Skills required: Enjoy working with the public; ability to communicate effectively with people of all ages; computer experience preferred; valid driver's license.

Access to restroom facilities: There are restroom and shower facilities in each of the park's campground areas.

How often do volunteers need to work on site? Volunteer's responsibilities will vary at each site, with a minimum of 25 hours per week. Also, volunteers must be available to campers who are in need of assistance during holidays and when park offices are closed.

Tools and equipment provided: Tools, equipment, and cart will be provided as needed. We will provide personal protective equipment as needed and instruct in proper use.

Volunteer Application Deadline: Must be submitted a minimum of two weeks prior to Campground Host assignment. Volunteers need to complete the Volunteer Application, which requires a background check.

Orientation/Training: Campground hosts will receive orientation and training prior to their first night's stay and continue as needed.

Restrictions: Must reside at designated site only. Hosts will not have free access to any other park amenities.

Extra comments: This is a great opportunity for individuals who are traveling on a budget and are planning on an extended stay in South Florida. This volunteer position provides a great venue to share your experience and creativity and to help develop camping-related outdoor activities and programs such as campfire storytelling, boating excursions, and fishing instruction.

All RV sites include grill, electricity, water, and sewer hookups, except for Quiet Waters Park, where there is access to a water hookup and electricity only.

Platform tent camping (Quiet Waters Park only) includes water, electricity, grill and fire ring.

Dixie County

Cheyenne Stemple, Administrative Assistant/Grant Coordinator

Dixie County

P.O. Box 2600

Cross City, FL 32628

(352) 498 1426 Office

(352) 498 1277 Fax

clstemple@att.net

http://parks.dixie.fl.gov/?page_id=5

In response to our email:

Here in Dixie County we do welcome Volunteer Campground Host.

We have a total of 10 parks/boat ramps that provide space for Volunteer Host, 7 of these parks/boat ramps have Host already. We only have one Host per park.

The County offers electricity, water and sewer

There is no specific length of RV.

We do no track hours of the host, we just expect the host to look out for the County Property as if it was their own.

The Volunteers that we have stay year around at the park.

*Dtrac Park

4562 SW Hwy 358

Jena, FL 32359

Has Electric and Restroom

Needs a Park Host as of 08/01/2014

*Glen Dyals Park

21354 SE Hwy 349

Suwannee, FL 32692

Has Electric and Restroom

Needs a Park Host as of 08/01/2014

Gornto Springs Park/Boat Ramp

2463 NE 816th Ave.

Old Town, FL 32680

8 Camping Spots, Electric, Restroom, Shower and Pavilion

Current Host: Vertie Davis (352) 542-2689

Hinton Landing Park/Boat Ramp

119 SE 230th Ave.

Old Town, FL 32680

4 Camping Spots, Electric, Restroom, Shower and Pavilion

Current Host: Wesley Keen (352) 542-1287

Horseshoe Beach Park/Boat Ramp

244 8TH Ave W

Horseshoe, FL 32648

8 Camping Spots, Electric, Restroom and Pavilion

Current Host: Ms. Willie (352) 498-2935

Joe Anderson Park/ Boat Ramp

113 SE 155th Ave

Old Town 32680

Only 1 Night Camping, Electric, Restroom, Pavilion

Current Host: Bill Holland (352) 210-9524

Purvis Landing Park/Boat Ramp

294 NE 832nd St.

Old Town, FL 32680

Has Restroom and Pavilion

Current Host: Jack Bowen (352) 542-7650

Shired Island Park/Boat Ramp

11072 SE Hwy 357

Horseshoe, FL 32648

12 Camping Spots, Electric, Restroom, Shower and Pavilion

Current Host: Herbert Cannon (352) 498-0009

Turner Point Park/Boat Ramp

886 NE 453 Ave.

Old Town, FL 32680

Has Restroom and Pavilion

Now has a Park Host as of 08/01/2014

Waldo Park

1950 NE 389 Ave

Old Town, FL 32680

Has Electric, Restroom and Pavilion

Current Host: Shane Whiteeagle (352) 542-2803

Duval County

Daisy A. Biggs, Executive Assistant

Division of Natural and Marine Resource

Department of Parks, Recreation and Community Services

214 North Hogan Street, 3rd Floor

Jacksonville, FL 32202

(904) 255-7913

Jaxparks@coj.net

http://www.jaxparks.com

http://www.coj.net/departments/employee-services/volunteer-services/rcs-wfm-campground-host-hanna-park.aspx

http://www.coj.net/departments/employee-services/volunteer-services/rcs-wfm-campground-host-huguenot-park.aspx

Kathryn Abbey Hanna Park:

500 Wonderwood Dr.

Atlantic Beach, FL 32233

(904) 249-4700

http://www.coj.net/departments/parks,-recreation-and-community-services/recreation-and-community-programming/kathryn-abbey-hanna-park.aspx

How many campground hosts do you have at one time at each campground?

4-7

What kind of amenities do you offer your volunteer campground hosts? (Water, Sewers on site, Electric-20/30/50Amp, free laundry, free ice, free firewood, etc.)

Hosts are given a free campsite with water, sewer, electric-20/30/50Amp, and free ice

Is there a RV Rig Length limit at any of the campgrounds?

45'

How many hours per week do you require each campground host to put in?

The requirement is 20 hours per week per person (a couple would do 40 hours).

What, if any, time of the year do you have problems getting volunteers?

Summer is generally a challenge.

Length of Stay Limits

3 to 6 months

Huguenot Memorial Park:

10980 Heckscher Dr.

Jacksonville, FL 32226

(904) 251-3335

http://www.coj.net/departments/parks,-recreation-and-community-services/recreation-and-community-programming/huguenot-memorial-park.aspx

How many campground hosts do you have at one time at each campground?

Huguenot (1), Alimacani (3) that work at Huguenot

What kind of amenities do you offer your volunteer campground hosts? (Water, Sewers on site, Electric-20/30/50Amp, free laundry, free ice, free firewood, etc.)

20/30/50 AMP electricity, water, sewer

Is there a RV Rig Length limit at any of the campgrounds?

30' at Huguenot & unlimited at Alimacani

How many hours per week do you require each campground host to put in?

20 for regular hosts (2 each) and 25 for lead hosts (2 each)

What, if any, time of the year do you have problems getting volunteers?

Currently have returning hosts for summer and winter schedules and are not looking to fill any. Schedules run from Nov – Mar & Apr – Oct (As of June 2014)

Length of Stay Limits

3 to 6 months

Escambia County

Michael E. Rhodes, Escambia County Parks and Recreation

1651 East Nine Mile Rd

Pensacola, Florida 32514

(850) 475-5220

MERHODES@co.escambia.fl.us

http://www.myescambia.com/government/departments/parks

In response to our email:

We have a Campground Caretaker and a Campground Host

The Caretaker gets a free place (trailer) to stay and a gets a very, very, very minimal stipend. He is responsible for mowing and general upkeep of the facility.

The Camp Host essentially is the caretakers back up man or woman. *The host gets a complimentary campground space but no amenities are provided nor is there any pay but he or she may serve as back up to the caretaker in the check in office or when caretaker is away.*

No certain hours for host or caretaker. *We ask campers to check out after 7AM or check in before 7 PM, thus they are not banging on the door early or late.*

Right now we are in good shape for our caretaker and camp host. (as of June 2014)

Lake Stone Campground

801 West Highway 4

Century, FL 32535

(850) 256-5555

http://www.myescambia.com/government/departments/parks/lakestone

Gilchrist County

209 S.E. 1st St

Trenton, FL 32693

(352) 463-3198

http://gilchrist.fl.us/

Hart Springs

Mitchell Gentry - Park Manager/Volunteer Coordinator

4240 SW 86th Ave

Bell, FL 32619

Fax: 352-463-3468

Phone: 352-463-3444

fun@hartsprings.com

http://www.hartsprings.com

http://www.hartsprings.com/volunteer.php

Spoke to Mr. Gentry and he stated that they have volunteer positions but are currently filled up for the foreseeable future. You can send in your resume and should an opening ever come up he would be more than happy to consider it. However, they placed an advertisement on **our favorite website** week of September 20, 2014 that states the following:

Hart Springs Park and Campgrounds in Bell, Florida, is looking for RVers to serve as campground hosts. Located approx. 40 miles west of Gainesville, Florida.

Campground Host fulltime year round and a springs/park attendant on Sundays and evenings. Full Hookup 30/50, water and Sewer in exchange for park duties. Please call Mitchell @ 352-463-3444 or email us at fun@hartsprings.com.

Otter Springs

Debbie Destin/Kathy Richardson, Volunteer Coordinators

6470 SW 80th Ave

Trenton, FL 32693

(352) 463-0800

info@ottersprings.com

www.ottersprings.com

Per Gilchrist County website they only manage Hart Springs but per Otter Springs website they are managed by Gilchrist County in cooperation with Suwannee River Water Management District.

There is an application to fill out as well as a background check that is done for all potential park/campground hosts.

No. of Campground/Park Hosts: 4

Campsite Amenities: Water/Electric/Sewer

Electrical Types: 30/50Amps

RV/Trailer Rig length limits: None

Required Hours: 20 hours per week

Length of Stay: 4 months at a time, Volunteer must leave for at least a day and can come back for another 4 months.

Examples of Duties: Campground Host Duties, mechanic, carpentry, gardening, etc. They try to match the skills of the volunteers with the needs of the park.

Gulf County

Lynn Lanier, Deputy Administrator

Gulf County BOCC

1000 Cecil G. Costin Sr., Blvd.

Port St. Joe, FL 32456

Office: (850) 229-6106   Cell: (850) 227-8973   Fax: (850) 229-9252

llanier@gulfcounty-fl.gov

In response to our email:

For instance, which parks have volunteer campground hosts?

Only one park, Dead Lakes Park has camping facilities.

How many campground hosts do you have at one time at each campground?

We have one volunteer host at this campground.

What kind of amenities do you offer your volunteer campground hosts? (Water, Sewers on site, Electric-20/30/50Amp, free laundry, free ice, free firewood, etc.)

We allow him to park his RV in one of our spots to compensate him for his work.

Is there a RV Rig Length limit at any of the campgrounds?

I believe we can accommodate most sizes in certain lots designated.

How many hours per week do you require each campground host to put in?

Our host monitors cleanliness of restrooms, laundry facilities, showers, trash as well as making sure campers pay their fees, have everything they need, etc. No minimum amount of hours required.

What, if any, time of the year do you have problems getting volunteers?

We have been without volunteers at some points. However, we do have a maintenance crew that works for the county that assists in maintaining the facility when this happens.

Hamilton County

Hamilton County Parks and Recreation

4525 SW 107th Avenue

Jasper, FL 32052

Phone: (386) 792-3098

Phone: (386) 792-0663

Fax: (386) 792-0899

recreation@windstream.net

Gibson Park

6884 SW CR 751

Jasper, FL 32052

(386) 792-1631

Offers rustic camping or RV hookups, fishing and canoeing.

http://www.hamiltoncountyflorida.com/cd_parksrec.aspx

Volunteer Campground Host at Gibson Park but it is a permanent position and has been filled for over 4 years. Does not anticipate that there will be an opening anytime soon. Please contact the county Department of Parks and Recreation Department for more information.

Hillsborough County

Jason Chilson

Chilsonj@hillsboroughcounty.org

(813) 987-6284

Edward Medard Regional Park

6140 Edward Medard Parkway

Plant City, FL 33567

(813) 757-3802

http://www.hillsboroughcounty.org/Facilities/Facility/Details/Edward-Medard-Regional-Park-7933

Potential applicants will need to come by the park and pick up an application packet. They use volunteer campground hosts mainly during the late fall to early spring months as it is too hot and not very busy during the summer months. Contact the manager on site with any further questions.

E.G. Simmons Regional Park

2401 19th Ave NW

Ruskin, FL 33570

(813) 671-7655

http://www.hillsboroughcounty.org/Facilities/Facility/Details/EG-Simmons-Regional-Park-7932

Joey, the senior manager, states that they use volunteers primarily during the late fall early spring months. He does have regular volunteers already in place for six months at a time. But you can always call to have an application package sent for future consideration in case someone doesn't wish to return.

Lee County

Lee County Parks & Recreation

3410 Palm Beach Blvd

Fort Myers, FL 33916

(239) 533-7275

LeeParks@leegov.com

http://www.leeparks.org

Caloosahatchee Regional Park

19130 North River Rd

Alva, FL 33920

(239) 694-0398

http://www.leeparks.org/Facility_info?Project_num=0253

In response to our email:

Number of Campground Host Positions:

We have 2 sites for Hosts

Campsite Amenities for the Campground Hosts:

We do offer sewage hook-up, water, and electricity.

RV/Trailer Rig Length Limits:

We can accommodate 30-40 foot RVs.

Other Amenities for Campground Hosts:

We do offer ice, showers, firewood. Each site also has a concrete pad, picnic table, fire-ring and BBQ grill. We also can offer access to the Caloosahatchee River the campground hosts can bring a boat, canoe, or kayaks.

General Duties and Trailing Provided to Campground Hosts:

General Campground Host duties like cleaning bathhouses, campsites, camping area, answering camper questions, etc. We offer training on site for usage of vehicles, i.e.: golf cart, ATVs. And, use of power equipment: mowers, tractors, chainsaws, etc.

Times Volunteers Needed Most:

We currently have both of our sites occupied for the summer, which is a first. We have only had Hosts during the season November-April, when we are the busiest.

Yvonne Murray-Lewis, Parks and Recreation Sr. Program Specialist

East District Lee County

Caloosahatchee Regional Park

19130 North River Rd

Alva, FL. 33920

Office: (239) 694-0398

Cell: (239) 634-6307

YMurray-Lewis@leegov.com

Leon County

Leigh Davis - Director

Leon County Division of Parks and Recreation

2280 Miccosukee Road

Tallahassee, Florida 32308

Office: (850) 606-1470

Fax: (850) 606-1471

https://www.leoncountyfl.gov/parks/camping.asp

Hall Landing

2997 Luther Hall Rd

Tallahassee, FL 32310

Williams Landing

951 Williams Landing Rd

Tallahassee, FL 32310

In response to our email for information:

How many Campground Host Positions at each of the County Camping Areas?

LCPR has 2 Host Positions, one at Halls Landing, one at Williams Landing

What kinds of duties will each position be doing, in general?

General restroom detail, litter removal, providing information, assist with registration

How many hours per week do you require?

LCPR feels that the basic tasks take about 20 hours per week, with the expectation that a presence in the park be maintained.

Do the volunteer sites have electric (what kind 20/30/50Amp)/water/sewer on each site and if no sewer is there a dump station?

Sites include a 30 Amp Service, Sewer Hookup, Basic Phone for emergencies.

Is there a RV Rig Length Limit on any of volunteer sites?

We have accommodated longer 5th wheel type RV's. Access should not be an issue

What other amenities do you offer these volunteers? (free laundry, firewood, discounts, etc.)

None at this time

Are there any times of the year harder than others to get volunteers and if so, when?

We maintain a rotating list, we seldom have more than a week or two without a host. We require background screening on our volunteers at our cost.

Who should a potential volunteer contact for more information? (Name, Phone Number and email address)

Leon County Parks and Recreation

(850) 606-1470

Josh McSwain

mcswainj@leoncountyfl.gov

Marion County

Gina Peebles, CPRP - Marion County Parks and Recreation Director

111 SE 25 Ave

Ocala, FL 34471

Office: (352) 671-8555

Cell: (352) 817-3388

Fax: (352) 671-8550

Gores Landing

13750 NE 98 St

Ft. McCoy, FL 32134

(352) 671-8560

http://www.marioncountyfl.org/departments-agencies/department-a-z/parks-and-recreation/parks-directory-list-table-list/-selamenityid-8

In response to our email:

Marion County Parks and Recreation has one campground, Gores Landing. We just found someone to be our host camper, so I don't expect to need anyone for several months (if not longer).

We do provide our host camper free electric/water/septic hookup in exchange for general park duties (educating users of rules, acting as an emergency point of contact, restroom cleaning and trash pickup to name a few general duties).

Martin County

Joseph Pilla, Phipps Park Supervisor

Parks and Recreation Department

Martin County Board of County Commissioners

Phipps Park Campground

2175 SW Locks Rd

Stuart, FL 34997

(772) 287-6565

772-287-6565

jpilla@martin.fl.us

Volunteer Information for Martin County

http://www.martin.fl.us:7778/portal/page?_pageid=354,422060&_dad=portal&_schema=PORTAL

Phipps Park Campground Webpage

http://www.martin.fl.us:7778/portal/page?_pageid=354,3251499&_dad=portal&_schema=PORTAL

In response to our email:

Which parks have volunteer campground hosts?

Phipps Park Campground is the only County facility with such.

How many campground hosts do you have at one time at each campground?

Currently we have three Camp Hosts on staff.

What kind of amenities do you offer your volunteer campground hosts? (Water, Sewers on site, Electric-20/30/50Amp, free laundry, free ice, free firewood, etc.)

Two of our Hosts sites have FHU/50 amp service. One site has water and electric only.

Is there a RV Rig Length limit at any of the campgrounds?

No.

How many hours per week do you require each campground host to put in?

Twenty-five hours.

What, if any, time of the year do you have problems getting volunteers?

During the summer months.

Orange County

Orange County Parks and Recreation

4801 West Colonial Dr.

Orlando, FL 32808

(407) 836-6200

parks@ocfl.net

Download the Orange County Florida Parks and Recreation Camping Booklet

http://www.orangecountyfl.net/Portals/0/Library/Culture-Recreation/docs/Camping%20at%20Orange%20County%20Parks.pdf

Clarcona Horse Park

3535 Damon Rd

Apopka, FL 32703

(407) 886-6255

http://www.orangecountyfl.net/CultureParks/Parks.aspx?m=dtlvw&d=10#.U8XhMfldWQY

Bobby Hogue, Manager – must come by the park and pick up an application packet. There is a background check for each volunteer. Basically, most volunteers stay about 6 months to a year.

Kelly Park/Camp Joy

400 East Kelly Park Rd

Apopka, FL 32712

(407) 254-1901

http://www.orangecountyfl.net/CultureParks/Parks.aspx?m=dtlvw&d=22#.U8XhbfldWQY

Terri Probst, Manager – must come by the park and pick up an application packet. There is a background check for each volunteer. Volunteers can stay anywhere from 4 months to a year at a time. One position for Kelly Park and another one for Camp Joy.

Magnolia Park

2929 South Binion Rd

Apopka, FL 32703

(407) 886-4231

http://www.orangecountyfl.net/CultureParks/Parks.aspx?m=dtlvw&d=26#.U8Xhsfld WQY

Spoke to an employee named Fred who stated that they have regular volunteers for the whole year. One stays for 6 months and the other two split the remaining time at 3 months each. He does not anticipate any of them not returning every year. But you can always contact the park and ask to have an application packet mailed for future consideration.

Moss Park

12901 Moss Park Rd

Orlando, FL 32832

(407) 254-6840

http://www.orangecountyfl.net/CultureParks/Parks.aspx?m=dtlvw&d=29#.U8Xh0vld WQY

Eric Ness – Manager (407) 722-1614– usually takes applications for new volunteers in September for the late fall to early spring months. It is best to drop by the park during the week and pick up the application package. There is a background check to be done and he will make assignments for the coming year from there.

Palm Beach County

Palm Beach County Parks and Recreation Department

Administrative Offices

2700 6th Avenue South

Lake Worth, Florida 33461-4799

(561) 966-6600

http://www.pbcgov.com/parks/

Volunteer With Us!

(561) 966-7066

parksvol@pbcgov.org

http://www.pbcgov.com/parks/jobs/volunteering/#.U8Xjf_ldWQY

pbcparkrangers@pbcgov.org

John Prince Park Campground

4759 South Congress Ave.

Lake Worth, Florida 33461

(561) 582-7992 Toll Free: (877) 992-9925

http://www.pbcgov.com/parks/camping/johnprincepark/

Potential volunteers will need to keep checking the website for any openings. As of this printing there was no listing for volunteers for this park. The application for volunteering is online.

http://www.pbcgov.com/parks/jobs/volunteering/johnprincecamp.htm

Peanut Island Campground

6500 Peanut Island Rd.

Riviera Beach, FL 33404

(561) 845-4445 Toll Free: (866) 383-5730

http://www.pbcgov.com/parks/peanutisland/campground.htm#.U8XihvldWQY

There is one position online listed for this campground with contact information.

Peanut Island Campground

Intracoastal Waterway, near the Lake Worth Inlet, Riviera Beach, FL 33404

Contact: David Salvador, (561) 845-4445

Campground Attendant

Thursday-Sunday evening and day shifts.

The ideal person for this position will love everything about the marine environment and provide excellent customer service.

Ability to Track campsite availability

Recognize and resolve maintenance problems

Perform arithmetic computations and prepare accurate financial reports

Effectively communicate and provide courteous customer service to a very diverse clientele

Interpret, learn, execute, relay, follow, and enforce County rules, regulations, policies, and procedures

Make diverse, timely, and accurate decisions which complies with appropriate policies and procedures while under pressure and in a confined area

Knowledge of office practices and procedures

Contact the park directly for more information about the above position and any others they may have coming available in the future.

http://www.pbcgov.com/parks/jobs/volunteering/peanutislandcamp.htm

South Bay RV Campground

100 Levee Rd.

South Bay, Florida 33493

Office Phone: (561) 992-9045

Toll Free: (877) 992-9915

http://www.pbcgov.com/parks/camping/southbay/#.U8XiovldWQY

There was one volunteer position listed on the website and again you will need to contact the park directly to get information from the coordinator about this position and any others that may be available.

South Bay RV Campground

100 Levee Road, South Bay, FL 33493

Contact: L.J. Margolis, (561) 992-9067

Campground Attendant

Do you like working outdoors and meeting new people...then Parks is for you! Volunteers at South Bay RV Campground will assist campground staff with several campground maintenance tasks such as litter pick-up, sweeping, vegetation removal, raking, restroom cleaning, minor carpentry projects, answering phones, assisting the public, etc. All volunteers will participate in volunteer orientation prior to working at the campground. Orientation will include volunteer welcome package, review of dress codes and safety procedures and general campground information/tour. Assignments are provided by the volunteer supervisor.

Shifts Available

Variable hours - contact site for more details

http://www.pbcgov.com/parks/jobs/volunteering/southbaycamp.htm

Pasco County

Frederick J. Buckman, Director of Parks and Recreation

Pasco County Parks and Recreation

4111 Land O' Lakes Blvd. Suite 202

Land O' Lakes, FL 34639

Phone: (813) 929-2760

Fax: (813) 929-2758

fbuckman@pascocountyfl.net

http://www.pascocountyfl.net/index.aspx?NID=252

Volunteer Pasco County

http://fl-pascocounty.civicplus.com/index.aspx?NID=1976

Crews Lake Wilderness Park

16739 Crews Lake Dr.

Spring Hills, FL

(727) 861-3038

http://www.pascocountyfl.net/index.aspx?NID=305

(Primitive Tent Camping)

In response to our email:

I am the Park site supervisor at Crews Lake Park in Spring Hills. Currently, we do not have a space for a host camper right now. We do have plans in the near future for 5 RV sites with electric and water plus a sewer dump station. We are hoping to be complete by September 2014. At that time I would surely entertain the idea of having a host on site.

David A. Jay

djay@pascocountyfl.net

Withlacoochee River Park

12449 Withlacoochee Blvd.

Dade City, FL

(352) 567-0264

http://www.pascocountyfl.net/index.aspx?NID=303

(Primitive Tent Camping and RV Camping)

Operated by Pasco County, land owned by South West Florida Water Management District

I spoke to one of the employees named Joe about any volunteer positions on August 25, 2014 and he stated that they have just recently added new campsites to the park. However, they have to wait until the campground gets more visitors before they will be able to petition the county to create volunteer campground host positions. This may take some time but they are definitely planning to add them in the future.

Pinellas County

Chris Muhrlin, Chief Park Ranger

Pinellas County Parks & Conservation Resources

Fort De Soto Park

3500 Pinellas Bayway S

Tierra Verde, FL, 33715

727-552-1862

cmuhrlin@pinellascounty.org

Fort Desoto

3500 Pinellas Bayway South

Tierra Verde, FL 33715

(727) 893-9185 or (727) 552-1862

http://www.pinellascounty.org/park/05_ft_desoto.htm

In response to our email:

Which parks have volunteer campground hosts?

Fort De Soto Park is the only Pinellas County Park that has a campground and utilizes camp hosts.

How many campground hosts do you have at one time at each campground?

During the winter months Fort De Soto campground will staff as many as 9 couples working as camp hosts. During the summer months it will vary between 3 to 5 couples.

What kind of amenities do you offer your volunteer campground hosts? (Water, Sewers on site, Electric-20/30/50Amp, free laundry, free ice, free firewood, etc.)

The amenities we offer our camp hosts is free admission into the park, their campsite for the duration of their stay (which includes water and electric 20/30/50amp), we do not have on site sewer hook-ups, however; we have two separate dump stations, which are located on the premises. Unfortunately, we do not offer free amenities such as laundry, ice or firewood, because these items are made available for purchase by a privately contracted concessionaire.

Is there a RV Rig Length limit at any of the campgrounds?

Most of our RV campsites will accommodate a 40 foot rig, although an RV larger than 40 feet could possibly become an issue.

How many hours per week do you require each campground host to put in?

We require our camp host to work, 40 hours per week (20 hours each as a couple) and as a single person – 36 hours per week.

What, if any, time of the year do you have problems getting volunteers?

The summer months are our most difficult time for recruiting camp hosts, however, we have a waiting list for the Fall, Winter and Spring months.

Sarasota County

Carolyn Brown, Parks and Recreation Director

Sarasota County Parks and Recreation

1660 Ringling Blvd

Sarasota, Florida 34236

(941) 861-5000

cnbrown@scgov.net

https://www.scgov.net/parks/Pages/default.aspx

Volunteer Sarasota County

General Volunteer Questions:

Vickie French, Volunteer Program Coordinator

1660 Ringling Blvd. 1st Floor

Sarasota, FL 34236

(941) 650-1292

vfrench@scgov.net

https://www.scgov.net/Volunteer/Pages/default.aspx

Response to our Email Inquiry:

Tricia Wisner, Business Development Coordinator

Sarasota County Parks and Recreation

Phone: (941) 861-5515

Cell: (941) 993-9720

pwisner@scgov.net

We are just preparing to launch our first campground host program. We are still working out the position details and hope to have something out in about 3 weeks. (June 18, 2014)

Turtle Beach Campground

8862 Midnight Pass Rd

Sarasota, FL, 34242

Phone: (941) 349-3839

turtlebeachcampground@scgov.net

https://www.scgov.net/TurtleBeachCampground/Pages/default.aspx

Spoke to Tricia Wisner, 08/04/2014, still waiting on county approval for the volunteer campground host positions at Turtle Beach Campground. Once approved will email all those who have inquired about the position to start the application process. She is looking for 4 to 6 month commitments and hopes to have two positions each cycle and booking assignments at least a year in advance. Check out the campground's webpage for more information about the park and the camping amenities.

St. Lucie County

St. Lucie County Parks and Recreation

2300 Virginia Ave

Fort Pierce, FL 34982

(772) 462-1522

http://www.stlucieco.gov/parks/

Savannas Park and Campground

1400 Midway Rd

Fort Pierce, FL 34982

Office: (772) 464-7855

Fax: (772) 464-1765

Toll Free: (800) 789-5776

http://www.stlucieco.gov/parks/savannas.htm

Savannas@stlucieco.gov

Spoke to park personnel and was told they are booked solid for the foreseeable future. She has had the same volunteers for over 10 years but if you would still like to put in an application you have to contact the park directly and speak to the coordinator.

Wakulla County

Cody Solburg, Director

Wakulla County Parks and Recreation

79 Recreation Dr.

Crawfordville, FL 32327

csolburg@mywakulla.com

http://www.mywakulla.com/departments/parks/index.php

Dolly Mitchell, Park Attendant

79 Recreation Dr.

Crawfordville, FL 32327

(850) 926-7227

dmitchell@mywakulla.com

Office: (850) 926-7227

Fax: (850) 926-1083

Volunteer Wakulla County Park and Recreation

http://www.mywakulla.com/departments/communications_and_public_services/departments/volunteer.php

Newport Park

8046 Coastal Hwy

St. Marks, FL 32355

850-926-7227

http://www.mywakulla.com/departments/parks/newport_campground.php

They do have one volunteer campground host but it is considered a semi-permanent position. They will advertise when it becomes available again

FLORIDA STATE FORESTS

The Florida State Forests are governed by the Florida Department of Agriculture. And as such they have a different volunteer program structure, time limits, accommodations and sometimes different kinds of duties. There are currently 35 different Florida State Forests but only a few of them have the resources to accommodate campers or even live on-site volunteers. We hope that this changes in the future. The website states there are only 4 state forests that currently offer campground/park hosts volunteer sites. We contacted all of state forests to find out if they plan on adding any in the future and to confirm the information for the ones listed that already do.

If you are interesting in applying for any of these positions please contact the people below. You will have to fill out an application, pass a background screening and have several references. For those new to Workamping you really need to visit the forests ahead of time, meet the park rangers, and look over the area to be sure you want to be there for the time you agree to stay. Most state forests are out-of-the-way places and do not get cellphone service or local TV service of any kind.

As I stated earlier the Florida Department of Agriculture who manages the Florida State Forests does not necessarily have a time limit or length of stay limits for their volunteers. You will have to contact the State Forest you are interested in helping to find out more. The length of stay can change depending on the season, unforeseen circumstances, skills the volunteer has and past performances of other volunteers.

We have only listed those that have a live on-site program in place or have agreed to talk further about having people volunteer. If you are familiar with the concept of "Boon-docking" and don't mind being without certain amenities for an extended period of time you may want to contact the other state forests to discuss the possibilities of being their "live on-site" volunteer.

http://www.freshfromflorida.com/Divisions-Offices/Florida-Forest-Service/Our-Forests/State-Forests

Blackwater River State Forest

David Creamer, Recreation Administrator

Blackwater River State Forest

11650 Munson Highway

Milton, FL 32570

(850) 957-6140 ext. 101

David.Creamer@freshfromflorida.com

http://www.freshfromflorida.com/Divisions-Offices/Florida-Forest-Service/Our-Forests/State-Forests/Blackwater-River-State-Forest

In response to our email:

We do have Campground Hosts/Hostesses living on site.

Bear Lake, Krul, Coldwater, Hurricane, Karick, Camp Paquette, and Bone Creek are the sites that have Volunteers living there.

Electric, water, with septic are offered

Most difficult time to find volunteers' is during the spring and summer months.

One area has a washing machine/dryer that was donated by a volunteer that had left. Some of the other areas have washers and dryers but they are brought in by the Campground Host/Hostess.

The amount of hours depends on the time of the year. It is much busier in the spring and summer than in the middle of winter. We have to make sure the work is getting done but the schedule is very flexible each day throughout the year. The work involves using a riding lawn mower, cleaning restrooms, picking up litter, answering questions from the public, etc. The restrooms need to be cleaned daily so it involves being on site 7 days a week unless the Volunteer is on vacation. We also like to have someone in the facility at night to keep an eye on the facilities.

Please visit the website for more information about these areas. You will need to contact the forest directly to find out when there are future openings for volunteers.

Bear Lake Campground

Campsites with electricity and water (some sites have water only, Restrooms and showers, Dining facility (reservations are required: Call (850) 957-6140), Boat ramps, Pier.

Bear Lake Recreation Area is located approximately 2.5 miles east of Munson off of Highway 4.

Bone Creek

Bone Creek is a Day Use area which includes a man-made pond with swimming area, dock, and picnic tables. Fishing is allowed in the lake except in the swimming area.

Bone Creek Recreation Area is located above Holt, Florida. The entrance sign to Bone Creek is located on Highway 90.

Camp Paquette

Camp Paquette is a youth facility with 2 bathrooms and an outdoor pavilion. There are 4 primitive camping areas with designated fire pits and picnic tables. There is a swimming lake in the back of the facility with a pier. Fishing is allowed outside of the swimming area.

Camp Paquette is located off of Belandville Road, due north of Munson, Florida approximately 6 miles above Highway 4

Coldwater Creek Campground

Horse stalls, Campsites with electricity and water, Restrooms and showers, Dining facility

Krul Recreation Area Campground

Swimming dock, Campsites with electricity and water, Restrooms and showers, Pier

Krul is located ½ mile east of Munson north of Highway 4.

North Hurricane Lake Campground

Campsites with electricity and water (some sites have water only), Restrooms and showers, Boat ramp, North Hurricane Lake Youth Area is a primitive camping area with restrooms nearby.

These recreation areas may be reached from Hurricane Lake Road off of Highway 4. They are located approximately 7 miles north of Highway 4 in north Okaloosa County. There is access to the south side primitive campground from Kennedy Bridge Road and access to the north side campground via Beaver Creek Highway.

North Karick Lake Campground and South Karick Lake Campground

In North Karick Lake Campsites there are campsites with electricity and water, Restrooms and showers, Boat ramp, Pier, North Karick Lake Youth Area is a primitive camping area with restrooms nearby. South Karick Lake Campsites with electricity and water, Restrooms and showers, Boat ramp

The campgrounds are located east of county road 189 approximately 7.5 miles north of Baker.

Cary State Forest

Devon McFall, Park Ranger

Cary State Forest

7465 Pavilion Dr.

Bryceville, FL 32209

(904) 266-5021 or (904) 266-5003   On weekends, (904) 266-5020

Devon.McFall@freshfromflorida.com

http://www.freshfromflorida.com/Divisions-Offices/Florida-Forest-Service/Our-Forests/State-Forests/Cary-State-Forest

Spoke to Devon McFall on 05/22/2014, he stated he doesn't have a campground host plan but would like to consider anyone willing to clean the bathhouse, restrooms, camping area, mow etc. There is well water from a shallow well but no electric in the camp, could use the office washer/dryer and some space in their office refrigerator, if you use a generator it has to be a quiet one. Of course, if your RV/Trailer rig has solar power that would be pretty terrific.

If you would like a unique volunteer experience and have a little plumbing, electric or just handyman experience they could really use your help. He requests that any potential volunteers contact him directly. He will conduct a preliminary phone interview, ask that you come in for a more formal interview and visit the forest. Then there is an application to fill out as well as a background check to be done before volunteers are accepted. If you are interested in botany and/or giving educational talks that is a plus. The forest doesn't have a recreational resource person to plan events right now.

Cary State Forest is the second oldest state forest in Florida. There is not a lot of funding for improvements to the recreational spaces within the forest and they could use an active "Friends Group" to organize some fundraisers to maybe dig a deep water well, put in some electric boxes in the campgrounds, and update the showers. There is no "water" feature within the forest to attract more visitors but there is a great potential for educational events with large wood pavilion filled with exhibits.

Three drive-up Semi Primitive Campsites are located on Cary State Forest. Campsite 1 accommodates 15 people, Campsite 2 accommodates 25 people and Campsite 3 accommodates 100 people. Water is available at campsite 3 only. A restroom facility with hot showers is provided for campers and day use visitors.

Pine Log State Forest

Joseph L. Sowell, Park Ranger

Pine Log State Forest

5583 Longleaf Rd

Ebro, FL 32437

(850) 535-2888

Joseph.sowell@freshfromflorida.com

http://www.freshfromflorida.com/Divisions-Offices/Florida-Forest-Service/Our-Forests/State-Forests/Pine-Log-State-Forest

A campground with 20 campsites can be found at the Pine Log State Forest Recreation Area. All sites are fully equipped with electric and water hook-ups. Restrooms with showers and a sanitary dumping station are located on site.

Spoke to Park Ranger Sowell, who stated that they had 1 campground host position. The State Forest positions do not have a length of stay limit, per se. It is strictly up to the volunteer and the park rangers. Generally, the volunteers are allowed to stay as long as they want so long as the park rangers are happy with their service. They have a current volunteer who will more than like stay until next spring. For those interested in volunteering should call back in February or March to schedule the upcoming service time.

The campground host has a free campsite with water and electric but needs drive over to the dump station or use a blue boy for sewer. They do not have a washer or dryer for the volunteers so you will need to go to the nearest town to wash your clothes. They only require about 20 hours per month for their volunteers and consists of cleaning campsites when they are emptied, cleaning the bathhouse and grounds and occasionally helping the forest rangers with grounds maintenance.

Tate's Hell State Forest

Marti Miller, Volunteer Coordinator

Tate's Hell State Forest

290 Airport Rd

Carrabelle, FL 32060

(850) 681-5950

Marti.Miller@FreshFromFlorida.com

http://www.freshfromflorida.com/Divisions-Offices/Florida-Forest-Service/Our-Forests/State-Forests/Tate-s-Hell-State-Forest

Located in the Walnut Creek Recreation Area

No. of Campground Hosts: 1

Campsite Amenities: Water/Electric/Sewer

Electrical Types: 30Amps

RV/Trailer Rig Length Limits: None

FREE Extras: Washer/Dryer

Other Park Amenities/Notes: None

Hours Required: 20 Hours or more depending on needs

Length of Stay: 2 month minimum, no maximum

Examples of Duties: Cleaning restroom, camping area, maintenance of grounds and facilities.

Times Year Volunteers Needed Most: summer months usually

Withlacoochee State Forest

Keith Mousel, Manager

Withlacoochee Forestry Center

15019 Broad St

Brooksville, FL 34601-4201

Phone: (352) 797-4101

Fax: (352) 797-4103

Keith.Mousel@FreshFromFlorida.com

http://www.freshfromflorida.com/Divisions-Offices/Florida-Forest-Service/Our-Forests/State-Forests/Withlacoochee-State-Forest

Cindy Hausman, Park Ranger

Cynthia.Hausman@freshfromflorida.com

Responded to my email:

At this point we have 1 site that will be vacant come fall and there are many applications on file to possibly fill that spot. We are looking for someone this summer at the Croom Motorcycle area who does not have a dog as a pet as we do not allow pets in this area. The campgrounds that are closed temporarily are closed due to budget constraints, not because of slowing occupancy. With our new budget starting July 1 we hope to open them back up. We offer 50amp at the sites and we have dump sites. As we are different than the state parks we do not offer the amenities they do. We require at least 24 hrs. of work volunteered per week and do not actually require a length of time. Most of our hosts come in Oct/Nov and leave March, April or May. We would like to have hosts during the summer but most are snow birds.

Please contact this forest directly to find out about future volunteer availabilities.

Citrus Tract

Holder Mine Recreation Campground

***27 Campsites with electric, water, picnic table and fire ring, 2 bathhouses, dump station

Mutual Mine Recreation Campground

***13 non-electric campsites with water, picnic table and fire ring, bathroom no shower

Tillis Hill Recreation Campground

***37 campsites with paved slabs, electric, water, picnic table and fire ring, 2 bathhouses, dump station

Croom Tract

Hog Island Recreation Campground

***20 non-electric campsites with water, picnic table and fire ring, restrooms and showers, dump station

River Junction Recreation Campground

***20 non-electric campsites with water, picnic table and fire ring, restrooms and showers

Silver Lake Recreation Area Complex

Silver Lake Campground

***23 campsites with electricity, water, picnic table and fire ring, restrooms and showers, dump station

Cypress Glen Campground

***34 campsites with electricity, water, picnic table and fire ring, restrooms and showers

Crooked River Campground

***26 non-electric campsites (Tent only) with picnic table and fire ring, restrooms and showers

Croom Motorcycle Area

Buttgenbach Mine Campground

***51 Campsites with electricity (50Amp), water, picnic table and fire ring, 2 Restrooms and Showers, Dump Station

OTHER STATE AGENCIES IN FLORIDA WITH CAMPGROUND/PARK HOST POSITIONS

Florida Fish and Wildlife

There are very few opportunities for RVers to volunteer with the Florida Fish and Wildlife in exchange for full-service campsites. Hopefully, that will change in the future. There are only about 10 Wildlife Management Areas in and around Florida that are managed by the FWC and another dozen or so that are managed in cooperation with other agencies in the state such as the Water Management Districts. Below is a listing of the current Volunteer Coordinators that you can contact to find out more information about the current and future opportunities available to us "Full-Time RVers" who would like to contribute to maintaining and/or restoring our natural resources here in Florida. If you are a naturalist, marine biologist or even just study wildlife as a hobby you might want to consider volunteering at one of your local wildlife management areas.

The positions we did find was advertised on a Workamping website. They are not advertised on the FWC's volunteer pages. The example below from Three Lakes WMA we found out about first from one of our fellow volunteers who stated that they were always looking for new live on-site volunteers during the winter months. The place is pretty secluded but it is located in south Florida. When we found the advertisement online we noticed that you have to call or write for more information.

In researching this book we emailed each of the WMA but didn't get a response and didn't have time to call each of them in turn. We did get a response from Mr. Murphy below who stated that he was going to research our request and get back to us. Sadly, he hasn't done it yet. If he should come up with some more information we will be sure and post it on our website.

Sharon Tatem, FWC Volunteer Program Manager

Sharon.Tatem@MyFWC.com

(850) 921-1047

Joe Murphy, North Central Region Volunteer Coordinator

Joseph.Murphy@MyFWC.com

(352) 754-6722

Jess Rodriguez, Northeast Region Volunteer Coordinator

Jess.Rodriguez@MyFWC.com

(352) 732-1225

Open Position, Southwest Region Volunteer Coordinator

(863) 648-3200

http://myfwc.com/get-involved/volunteer/

Examples of volunteer live on-site positions with the Florida Fish and Wildlife Department.

Volunteer at Herky Huffman / Bull Creek Wildlife Management Area

Volunteer work camping available at the Herky Huffman / Bull Creek Wildlife Management Area in Osceola County, Florida. This is a volunteer position with the Florida Fish and Wildlife Conservation Commission.

The Herky Huffman / Bull Creek Wildlife Management Area is approximately 23,500 acres located in central Florida that sits between the beaches of Melbourne and the theme parks of Orlando. The property is dominated by pine flatwoods and is excellent for hunting, fishing, birding, hiking, horseback riding, and biking.

We are looking for RVers to volunteer in exchange for full hook-up (water, electric, and septic) campsites. Volunteers are needed from the 6th of September, 2014, through the end of April, 2015.

Volunteer work includes checking hunters in and out of Herky Huffman/ Bull Creek Wildlife Management Area; answering hunters' questions; collecting biological data and samples from harvested game; and general maintenance on the Management Area.

Please send letter of interest to Jason Hickson, 5285 N. Kenansville Rd. St. Cloud, FL 34773, or via email to Jason.Hickson@MyFWC.com. Any questions please call Jason at (407) 498-0991. When you inquire about this work at a campground in Florida, be sure to specify that you saw the Help Wanted ad on Coleen's Workers On Wheels website. This job for RVers was posted in August 2014. Herky Huffman/ Bull Creek Wildlife Management Area - St. Cloud, Florida.

http://myfwc.com/viewing/recreation/wmas/cooperative/bull-creek/

****

Volunteer work at Three Lakes Wildlife Management Area, Kenansville, Florida.

Volunteer Work Camping for Florida Fish and Wildlife Conservation Commission at the Three Lakes Wildlife Management Area in rural Kenansville, Florida.

Three Lakes Wildlife Management Area volunteers are needed to man the hunter check station two days per week in exchange for full hook-up campsites. Volunteers are needed mid-September, 2013 through late-April, 2014 or any time within that period.

Volunteer duties includes checking hunters in and out of the Management Area, answering hunters' questions, collecting biological data and samples from harvested game and general maintenance on the Management Area.

The nearest cities include Saint Cloud, Melbourne, Kissimmee, and Vero Beach. Close to Disney, beaches, shopping, casinos, etc.

Please send letter of interest to Tina Hannon, 1231 Prairie Lakes Road, Kenansville, FL 34739 or call 407-436-1009. When you inquire about this volunteer work at the hunter check station, be sure to specify that you saw the Help Wanted ad on Coleen's Workers On Wheels website. This job for RVers was posted in August 2014. Three Lakes Wildlife Management Area, Kenansville, Florida.

http://myfwc.com/viewing/recreation/wmas/lead/three-lakes/

****Side note: If you would like a very reliable source of Workamping opportunities from all over the U.S. then Coleen's Workers on Wheels website is very good. We signed up for her email subscription service. Excellent. http://www.work-for-rvers-and-campers.com/*****

Florida Water Management Districts

There are five Water Management Districts located in Florida and they are charged with keeping our water and waterways clean, recharge the springs, have plans of action in case of floods or droughts and a host of other things involving the water supply in Florida. Over the years they have purchased a lot of land located along rivers, lakes and springs to help control growth, monitor toxins and allow us access to these lands for recreation and enjoyment.

Northwest Florida WMD

81 Water Management Drive

Havana, FL 32333

(850) 539-5999

http://www.nwfwater.com/

Response to our Email:

We do have a number of recreation areas and camp sites in our region but we do not staff any of these areas with Campground Hosts. All of our sites are very primitive with no hook-ups for water, sewer, electric, etc. The Florida Statutes require us to provide "low-impact, primitive recreational opportunities". Our campsites are primarily set up for tent camping (with a few camper/trailer spots). They are usually associated with small vessel boat ramps and/or public hunting areas. Our sites are primarily used by local hunters and fishers during their open seasons.

I do not believe we will be utilizing Campground Hosts in the very near future although it is something we have discussed in the past. We like the benefits of having someone monitor/protect/maintain our sites – especially in our vandalism prone areas. I also don't believe that many folks would be very interested in living at our primitive sites without any amenities other than our typical chemical portable toilets we have on site.

Thank you for your inquiry. Also… nice blog!

Steve L. Brown, Senior Lands Manager, West Region

Northwest Florida Water Management District

5453 Davisson Road

Milton, Florida 32583

Phone: (850) 626-3101

Fax: (850) 626-3110

We also got an email from the District Bureau Chief:

Our agency has a number of primitive campsites and a few primitive multi-site campgrounds. However, none of these facilities have water, sewer/septic, or electricity. Because of the lack of facilities and dispersed nature of the camp sites, we have not established a volunteer campground host program and have no immediate plans to do so. Please feel free to contact me if you have any additional questions about recreation opportunities on District lands. Thanks!

Sincerely,

Tyler L. Macmillan

Chief, Bureau of Land Management Operations

Northwest Florida Water Management District

81 Water Management Drive, Havana, Florida 32333-4712

(850) 539-5999; (800) 913-1518; FAX (850) 539-2777

Tyler.Macmillan@nwfwater.com

http://www.nwfwmd.state.fl.us

South Florida WMD

3301 GunClub Road

West Palm Beach, FL 33406-3089

(561) 686-8800

(800) 432-2045 (Florida only)

http://www.sfwmd.gov/portal/page/portal/sfwmdmain/home%20page

South Florida Water Management District does have volunteer campground host positions but were not really willing to share any information about where and how many there are. Below are the two emails we received in response to our inquiries:

Thank you for your email and it is a great idea to publicize the information on campgrounds and campground hosts.

There are a few campgrounds in the District property that have campground hosts provisions. I have sent your request to land managers for their input before I send you any info on this subject.

Bijaya Kattel, Ph.D.

Senior Recreation Planner

Land Stewardship Section (MS 5251)

South Florida Water Management District

3301 Gun Club Road

West Palm Beach, FL 33416

Phone: (561) 682-6640

Cell: (561) 329-6214

bjkattel@sfwmd.gov

Hi Jolene,

Please consider this email as a collective response to your emails to land managers in different areas of the South Florida Water Management District.

As I wrote earlier there are few sites that have provisions for campground hosts and we have volunteer campground hosts stationed at those sites. Unlike State Parks the campground hosts on District sites are multi-seasonal and are on site for more than one season, generally. Therefore, we are not looking for people at the moment but will keep your information handy should we have any opening(s) in the future.

Once again, thank you for your information and willingness to help on this subject.

Thanks,

Bijaya Kattel

(561) 682-6640

If you would like to pursue a live on-site position with one of the South Florida Water Management Districts camping areas it sounds like you will have to contact them directly.

St. Johns River WMD

P.O. Box 1429

Palatka, FL 32178-1429

(386) 329-4500

(800) 451-7106

http://floridaswater.com/

The St. Johns River Water Management District had a live on-site program but it has been discontinued. What a shame. There are some very nice recreational lands along the St. Johns River. Here is the email response from the District Chief:

We had campground hosts in the past to manage our game check duties for the hunt program. We no longer have game check stations, so we have ended that program.

Our camp sites are individual sites, not multiple site campgrounds, so there is no benefit for us to have camp ground hosts.

We have one site where we used to have a campground host to open and close gates from November to June, but we have been unable to secure a reliable host for that site and have ended that as well.

If you have additional questions, please feel free to contact me.

Steven R. Miller, Chief

Land Management Bureau

St Johns River Water Management District

(386) 329-4399

srmiller@sjrwmd.com

Suwannee River WMD

9225 CR 49

Live Oak, FL 32060

(386) 362-1001

(800) 226-1066 (Florida only)

http://www.srwmd.state.fl.us/

The Suwannee River Water Management District also doesn't use volunteer campground host or site hosts but they did give a lead into another place I can add to our listing!

Jolene,

We do not have a campground host program. We own several properties that are managed by other agencies utilize campground host.

The Suwannee River Wilderness Trail River Camps on District lands are managed by Florida State Parks and you can contact Jennifer Miller.

RO Ranch Equestrian Park

R.O. Ranch Visitors Center

10807 South State Road 51

Mayo, FL 32066

(386) 294-1475

Otter Springs Park & Campground

6470 SW 80th Avenue

Trenton, FL 32693

(352) 463-0800

Please let me know if you have additional questions.

Edwin McCook, Land Management Specialist

Suwannee River Water Management District

9225 CR 49

Live Oak, FL 32060

(386)647-3106 (Direct Line)

(386)362-1001, (800) 226-1066 (FL Only)

(386)362-1056 Fax

EJM@srwmd.org

http://www.mysuwanneeriver.com

The Suwannee River Wilderness Trail is listed above under the Florida State Parks. The Otter Springs Campground is listed under Gilchrist County Campgrounds but the RO Ranch Equestrian Park I did not know was located on Management Land and is operated in cooperation with Suwannee River WMD.

RO Ranch Equestrian Park

R.O. Ranch Visitors Center

10807 South State Road 51

Mayo, FL 32066

(386) 294-1475

http://www.roranch.org/

Spoke to an employee of the ranch and she stated that they do not have an "official" volunteer campground host program in place but have had volunteer campground hosts in the past and would be more than willing to consider them in the future. Please contact them directly via phone and/or you can send in your resume. The cover letter should include the dates you are hoping to volunteer and include current references from previous volunteer campground host assignments.

It would be a strictly volunteer position with a "Free" campsite as your only compensation. Those who are comfortable around horses would be an added plus. The duties, hours and length of stay will need to be discussed and agreed upon by both parties. It may also have to be brought before their board for approval as well.

NATIONAL AGENCIES

There are a few National Parks, Forest and other Agencies in the State of Florida and that offer Campground Host/Park Host opportunities. Since, we haven't had a chance to accept any of the Federal Park assignments, yet, we are not able to give any personal insight into being one. However, we have received emails and been offered opportunities in the past and have researched them for you. Some of them have campgrounds and others just have campsites for the volunteers. We hope you consider these as well. Most Federal placements require longer commitments from their volunteers but also offer other incentives such discounted propane or a monthly stipends. They also do not really like to post their listings more than a year in advance and most of these will be for the summer and early fall months. Your best bet is to sign-up with the http://www.volunteer.gov website which keeps a current listing of all the volunteer opportunities including campground hosts.

On the main page is a search box on the right where you look for current volunteer opportunities. There are several search boxes you can use to limit your search such as: keywords, city, state, agency, interests, housing/amenities, recent postings which is defaulted to "All", But I generally just choose "Florida" for the State and "RV/Trailer Pads" for the Housing/Amenities. And then hit the "Search" button. The descriptions of the jobs are pretty detailed and they give you the contact information for each of the posting. If you want to apply for any of the jobs you will have to fill out your application online.

National Forests

The U.S. Department of Agriculture manages our national forests and the resident volunteer hosts programs. Their requirements, length of stay, and amenities may different from other programs which have resident volunteers. All Federal government volunteers must first fill out an application online at: www.volunteer.gov. You will need to look at the existing and future openings on this website and apply to each position separately. It may take some time to hear back from these places as they receive a large number of applications all through the year. It wouldn't hurt to follow-up with the contact person for each application you filled out in a week or two.

There is a section on the application which asks if you would like your application forwarded to other Federal facilities with similar volunteer needs. If you would like a better chance of getting a volunteer position it would be best to say yes to this question. Once you get established as a reliable volunteer you should be able to contact each of the park facilities to let them know of your availability.

There is also a section at "Step 4" of the online application after filling in the months you are available, days of the week and number of hours that has an open text box labeled: "**This area is provided for more detailed responses**." This is a good place to list your references. Please give full name, contact phone number and email address if you have it. It is also called box 19. This will save the volunteer coordinator time when reviewing your application if they can go ahead and contact your references. A couple of the listings on the Volunteer.Gov website have this as a requirement when applying for one of their positions.

Apalachicola National Forest

Crystal Dillard, Volunteer Coordinator

Apalachicola National Forest

57 Taff Dr.

Crawfordville, FL 32327

(850) 575-9064 Ext: 6603

sddillard@fs.fed.gov

http://www.fs.usda.gov/main/apalachicola/home

Examples of Positions Available in the Apalachicola National Forest

Camel Lake Campground Host

Camel Lake is one of the beautiful camping and swimming recreation areas in the Apalachicola National Forest including day use picnicking, fishing and a hiking trail around the lake. The volunteer site hosts open and close the front gate daily, greet the visitors, remind visitors to pay entrance fees, daily check/clean facilities, restock paper supplies, empty trash receptacles, blow off paved parking areas and sidewalks, mow the lawn, weed eat during the warm months as needed, and clean grills and fire pits.

We at the Apalachicola National Forest do ask for a minimum of a 3 month or longer commitment

Our Camp Hosts are valued members of our community whose contributions are vital to the operation of the forest. Below is a list of the duties that our Camp Hosts perform:

*Welcome visitors and supply them with information about the forest.

*Perform general site maintenance and upkeep (e.g. picking up garbage, mowing the lawn, raking, cleaning out fire rings and grills, etc.).

*Clean and restock site restrooms.

*Monitor water quality and record data from flow and residual checks. Training will be provided.

*Assist the Recreation Technicians as needed. Depending on the site, this may include performing trail maintenance.

*Report maintenance issues and suspicious/inappropriate visitor activity to Forest Service staff members and/or law enforcement.

Camp Hosts should be able to complete the above duties either with or without reasonable accommodation. Camp Hosts must also be able to supply their own self-contained camping unit such as an RV, pull behind trailer, or fifth wheel trailer. Full hookups are available at most host sites.

To apply for a Camp Host position at the Apalachicola National Forest, you will need to fill out a volunteer application and submit at least three references. Please note, we conduct background checks on all applicants.

HOUSING & AMENITIES: Trailer/RV Pads

****

Fort Gadsden Volunteer Host

Fort Gadsden is the famous historic site along the timeless Apalachicola River, the western boundary of the Apalachicola National Forest. This recreation area includes a picnic pavilion and an interpretation exhibit center on the way to the grounds of the fort. Historical markers and interpretative kiosks/exhibits explain the history of the area. Visitors can then walk on the very ground where the Fort once stood, see the remains of the earth works, and peer out along the river and imagine the historic events that took place here in the past. The volunteer site host open and close the front gate daily, greet the visitors, daily check/clean facilities, restock paper supplies, clean picnic and exhibit areas, mow the lawn, weed eat during the warm months as needed, and empty trash receptacles.

We at the Apalachicola National Forest do ask for a minimum of a 3 month or longer commitment

Our Camp Hosts are valued members of our community whose contributions are vital to the operation of the forest. Below is a list of the duties that our Camp Hosts perform:

*Welcome visitors and supply them with information about the forest.

*Perform general site maintenance and upkeep (e.g. picking up garbage, mowing the lawn, raking, cleaning out fire rings and grills, etc.).

*Clean and restock site restrooms.

*Monitor water quality and record data from flow and residual checks. Training will be provided.

*Assist the Recreation Technicians as needed. Depending on the site, this may include performing trail maintenance.

*Report maintenance issues and suspicious/inappropriate visitor activity to Forest Service staff members and/or law enforcement.

Camp Hosts should be able to complete the above duties either with or without reasonable accommodation. Camp Hosts must also be able to supply their own self-contained camping unit such as an RV, pull behind trailer, or fifth wheel trailer. Full hookups are available at most host sites.

To apply for a Camp Host position at the Apalachicola National Forest, you will need to fill out a volunteer application and submit at least three references. Please note, we conduct background checks on all applicants.

HOUSING & AMENITIES: Trailer/RV Pads

****

Silver Lake Volunteer Host

Silver Lake is one of the beautiful day use swimming recreation areas in the Apalachicola National Forest including day use picnicking and fishing in non-motorized boats. The volunteer site hosts open and close the frost gate daily, stations themselves in the Gatehouse as time permits to greet the visitors, remind visitors to pay the entrance fees, give out information, daily check/clean facilities, restocking paper supplies, blow off paved parking areas and sidewalks, mow the lawn, weed eat during the warm months as needed, clean grills, and empty trash receptacles.

We at the Apalachicola National Forest do ask for a minimum of a 3 month or longer commitment

Our Camp Hosts are valued members of our community whose contributions are vital to the operation of the forest. Below is a list of the duties that our Camp Hosts perform:

*Welcome visitors and supply them with information about the forest.

*Perform general site maintenance and upkeep (e.g. picking up garbage, mowing the lawn, raking, cleaning out fire rings and grills, etc.).

*Clean and restock site restrooms.

*Monitor water quality and record data from flow and residual checks. Training will be provided.

*Assist the Recreation Technicians as needed. Depending on the site, this may include performing trail maintenance.

*Report maintenance issues and suspicious/inappropriate visitor activity to Forest Service staff members and/or law enforcement.

Camp Hosts should be able to complete the above duties either with or without reasonable accommodation. Camp Hosts must also be able to supply their own self-contained camping unit such as an RV, pull behind trailer, or fifth wheel trailer. Full hookups are available at most host sites.

To apply for a Camp Host position at the Apalachicola National Forest, you will need to fill out a volunteer application and submit at least three references. Please note, we conduct background checks on all applicants.

HOUSING & AMENITIES: Trailer/RV Pads

****

Springhill Motorcycle Trailhead Volunteer Host

Springhill Motorcycle Trailhead is a new reconstructed day-use area trailhead for OHV Motorcycle trails. The volunteer site hosts open and close the front gate daily, greet the visitors, remind visitors to pay entrance fees, daily check/clean facilities, restock paper supplies, blow off paved parking areas and sidewalks, mow the lawn, weed eat during the warm months as needed, rake the picnic area, and empty trash receptacles, and maintain the walking trails.

We ask for a minimum of a 3 month or longer commitment

Our Camp Hosts are valued members of our community whose contributions are vital to the operation of the forest. Below is a list of the duties that our Camp Hosts perform:

*Welcome visitors and supply them with information about the forest.

*Perform general site maintenance and upkeep (e.g. picking up garbage, mowing the lawn, raking, cleaning out fire rings and grills, etc.).

*Clean and restock site restrooms.

*Monitor water quality and record data from flow and residual checks. Training will be provided.

*Assist the Recreation Technicians as needed. Depending on the site, this may include performing trail maintenance.

*Report maintenance issues and suspicious/inappropriate visitor activity to Forest Service staff members and/or law enforcement.

Camp Hosts should be able to complete the above duties either with or without reasonable accommodation. Camp Hosts must also be able to supply their own self-contained camping unit such as an RV, pull behind trailer, or fifth wheel trailer. Full hookups are available at most host sites.

To apply for a Camp Host position at the Apalachicola National Forest, you will need to fill out a volunteer application and submit at least three references. Please note, we conduct background checks on all applicants.

HOUSING & AMENITIES: Trailer/RV Pads

Other Camping Areas that Might Have Volunteer Positions

*Hickory Landing, Sumatra, FL

*Wright Lake, Sumatra, FL – Volunteer Host always present per website

Ocala National Forest

Eve Shackleton, Volunteer Coordinator

Ocala National Forest

17147 E. Hwy 40

Silver Springs, FL 34488

(352) 625-2520

eshackleton@fs.fed.gov

http://www.fs.usda.gov/main/ocala/home

Examples of volunteer Positions Available with the Ocala National Forests

Campground Hosts

Description:

Campground hosts live on site and get a free full hook-up site for a volunteer provided RV in exchange for performing various duties. Hosts first and foremost represent the Forest Service and may be the first representative of the forest that a camper will encounter. Hosts must provide a pleasant and professional image to the visitors. Hosts also help maintain the campground by assisting with a variety of tasks which may include mowing, trash, restrooms- tasks vary by campground. Campground hosts also log in campers and provide Forest Service employee's information to ensure compliance is maintained. Some campgrounds have day use areas that the host also monitors.

This opportunity requires a 6 month commitment.

PLEASE PROVIDE REFERENCES AND THEIR CONTACT INFORMATION AT STEP 4 IN THE DETAILED RESPONSES BOX, FOR YOUR APPLICATION TO BE CONSIDERED

HOUSING & AMENITIES: Trailer/RV Pads

****

Trail Maintenance- Non-Motorized

Description:

Assist with the maintenance of the non-motorized trails (hiking, biking, equine) on the Ocala NF. Trail operations and maintenance may involve any of the following duties: mowing trails, hand pruning, chainsaw operation, removing logs and down trees, installation and repair of signs, grooming trails with mechanized equipment, closing trails, trailhead prevention contacts/visitor information, documenting issues on the trail and relaying information to trail manager. This position involves physically demanding field work at times and requires that the volunteer work in a variety of different ecosystems ranging from uplands to wetlands. Volunteers may also get caught in a variety of weather conditions (extreme hot, cold, rain, etc.). There are also a variety of stinging/biting insects and venomous snakes that may be encountered while working, as well as the potential for encountering various wildlife species, including black bears.

This position requires a 6 month commitment (Oct to Mar or Nov to Apr).

"PLEASE PROVIDE AT LEASET 3 REFERENCES AND THEIR CONTACT INFORMATION AT STEP 4, IN THE DETAILED RESPONSES BOX, FOR YOUR APPLICATION TO BE CONSIDERED

HOUSING & AMENITIES: Trailer/RV Pads

Description: Full hook up RV site for volunteer provided RV. No tents.

****

Visitor Centers

The position's primary duties involve operation and maintenance of the Ocala National Forest Visitor Centers. This position does not require on site residence. The goal is to keep the visitor centers open year round. Weekend & some holiday operation is the priority. Each visitor center (Ocklawaha and Pittman) operates similarly by providing visitor information and sales of merchandise such as maps, passes, shirts, books, etc. Visitor center hours are from 9am-4:30pm.

Duties include providing visitor information about the forest and surrounding area, operation of a cash register for sale of merchandise and passes, basic housekeeping, and coordinating with the visitor center manager on stock and other supply needs. This position requires a minimum 3 month commitment.

PLEASE PROVIDE REFERENCES AND THEIR CONTACT INFORMATION IN BLOCK #19 FOR YOUR APPLICATION TO BE CONSIDERED.

HOUSING & AMENITIES: Trailer/RV Pads

Description: Full hook up RV site if needed. Local volunteers welcome!

****

Recreation and Facility Maintenance

Description

Assist Forest Service staff and volunteers with the maintenance of recreation areas on the forest. Recreation maintenance personnel help keep our recreation areas beautiful and safe for our visitors. Duties include mowing, trash disposal, painting, restrooms, carpentry, and pressure washing. Recreation maintenance is a great way to see all of the recreation areas on the forest. Full hook-up sites available in exchange for 24 hours per week.

THIS OPPORTUNITY REQUIRES A 6 MONTH COMMITMENT. Please do not apply if you cannot meet a 6 month commitment.

PLEASE PROVIDE REFERENCES AND THEIR CONTACT INFORMATION IN BLOCK #19 FOR YOUR APPLICATION TO BE CONSIDERED.

HOUSING & AMENITIES: Trailer/RV Pads

****

Campgrounds within the Ocala National Forests that may have campground hosts:

*Alexander Springs Campground, Altoona, FL

*Big Bass Campground, Altoona, FL

*Clearwater Lake, Altoona, FL

*Delancy East, Salt Springs, FL

*Delancy West, Salt Springs, FL

*Fore Lake, Ocala, FL

Hopkins Prairie, Salt Springs, FL

*Juniper Springs Campground, Salt Springs, FL

*Lake Dorr, Umatilla, FL

*Lake Eaton, Ocala, FL

*River Forest

*Salt Springs Campground, Ocala, FL

Osceola National Forest

Debra Stucki, Volunteer Coordinator

Osceola National Forest

24874 US Hwy 90

Sanderson, FL 32087

(386) 752-2577 Ext: 4509

Dstucki02@fs.fed.gov

Examples of Volunteer Positions Available in the Osceola National Forest

Campground Hosts at Ocean Pond & Olustee Beach

Description: Campground Hosts

For a lucky few, the perfect camping option is serving as a volunteer campground host. The year-round, short-term post, which can last from six months to one year, offers a free campsite in exchange for 25 hours a week of work. Volunteer camp hosts greet visitors; perform general facility and groundskeeping maintenance. Ocean Pond is a serene and popular campground that provides 67 campsites with either electric, water or primitive set ups. Olustee Beach is a day use site with a fishing pier, boat ramp, beach and interpretive trails. Conveniently located between Jacksonville and Lake City, Florida it is a popular destination for both local visitors and traveling snowbirds.

HOST SITES STILL AVAILABLE NOW THROUGH SPRING 2015. WE PREFER A SIX MONTH STAY BUT WILL CONSIDER SHORTER TERMS.

The Osceola National Forest is within short driving distance to many popular attractions in Florida and some of the more popular north Florida cities, Jacksonville, Gainesville, St. Augustine and Tallahassee. Outdoor recreational activities are centered on Ocean Pond, a mile long lake that includes campgrounds, beaches, hiking, fishing, boating and swimming. OHV and equestrian trails along with undeveloped campgrounds are located around the forest. Other attractions include the Florida National Scenic Trail, Olustee Battlefield State Park and the Big Gum Swamp Wilderness.

To apply fill out an application with the dates of interest and relevant experience if any or email: dstucki02@fs.fed.us Check out our website. http://www.fs.usda.gov/osceola

HOUSING & AMENITIES: Trailer/RV Pads

Description: Will provide full hook - water, sewer and electric, propane reimbursement.

****

Visitor Depot Public Information

Description: Visitor Depot Public Information

Volunteers needed on the Osceola National Forest to man the Olustee Depot, a visitor center off of US Highway 90 in Olustee Florida. The Depot history dates back to the 1860s, where it played a significant role in serving as both a passenger and freight station during the Civil War and afterwards served as a hub for mail, supplies and people in the development of north Florida. Osceola is home to one of the largest reenactments in Florida the Olustee Battle which draws 20,000 visitors each year.

CAMPHOSTS NEEDED NOW THRU NEXT YEAR. SIX MONTH STAY PREFERED, BUT FLEXIBLE ON TIMING.

Volunteers will greet Forest Service visitors, provide information and sell books, collectibles and other Eastern National materials. Volunteers will maintain all aspects of the building (cleaning inside and outside the building, restrooms, mowing, maintaining the flower boxes) and also selling eastern national products. The Osceola NF is located about 45 minutes from Jacksonville, a major city, 40 minutes from Gainesville and the University of Florida and 20 minutes from Lake City, Florida with full amenities. The Osceola is close to the Atlantic Beaches, the Nature Coast which includes the many springs, caves and rivers that make up the area. Contact Debra : 386-752-2577 ext. 4509 // email : dstucki02@fs.fed.us

HOUSING & AMENITIES: Trailer/RV Pads

Description: Assignment includes a full hook-up, water electric, sewer, propane reimbursement and use of vehicle as available.

National Parks

Of course, our National Parks are governed by the National Park Service. In Florida, we have 11 National Parks designated and managed by the National Park Service. This includes a National Preserve, two National Seashores, two National Monuments, two National Memorials and one Ecological and Historic Preserve. Some of these are large enough to have camping areas and two of them have park hosts sites but no camping at all. You can check on the current openings at any of these National parks by frequently visiting the Volunteer Clearing House website: http://volunteer.gov

For those of us who are full-time RVers and have our own "self-contained" recreational vehicle we would select the state of "Florida" and the Housing/Amenities of "RV/Trailer Pads". These listings get updated on a regular basis. If you want to volunteer in South Florida in the Everglades, Big Cypress or even Biscayne Bay your best bet is to begin looking at the end of August. These three, generally, only have live on-site volunteer positions in the late fall and winter time. There are not too many hardy souls who would like to spend the late spring and summer months in this part of Florida, be they visitors or volunteers. So, the park rangers handle most of the cleaning and such during these times of the year. The national parks and forests in northern Florida have more of a "year round" volunteer needs listings.

Big Cypress National Preserve

Isobel Kalafarski, Volunteer Coordinator

Big Cypress National Preserve

33100 Tamiami Trail East

Ochopee, FL 34141-9710

(239) 695-4757

isobel_kalafarski@nps.gov

http://www.nps.gov/bicy/index.htm

Examples of Volunteer Positions Available at Big Cypress Preserve

Information Technology Team Volunteer

Description: Southern Florida in the winter and spring - wildlife abounds!

Qualifications: Background or general knowledge of personal computers using the Microsoft 7 operating system. Ability to interface with Preserve staff and provide basic maintenance support in the areas of software (Microsoft Office and Microsoft 7) and hardware support (basic diagnostics).

Duties: Provide basic end user IT support to preserve staff. Must turn in time sheets and use records to IT Supervisor on a monthly basis. Supervision will be provided by the senior member of the IT staff or the IT assistant, dependent on the situation.

Time Commitment Required: A single VIP must provide a minimum of 32 hours/week. If a couple is providing volunteer service, even if volunteering for different branches, they each must provide 24 hours/week for a total of 48 hours/couple/week.

Physical Demands: Periods of sitting, standing, walking, and bending. Also, may be carrying IT equipment weighing up to 20 lbs. over uneven, rough, or wet terrain.

Work Environment: Volunteer duties generally performed in an air-conditioned or heated building. However, some work may be performed outdoors in inclement weather.

Uniform: Volunteer will be issued three uniform shirts, a jacket, and a hat. Volunteer must supply khaki or dark brown pants, socks, and closed-toed shoes.

Services provided to Volunteer: RV site with full hook-ups. Use of the preserve headquarters laundry facilities and unheated outdoor swimming pool. May invite one set of guests to spend up to three nights on your site - they will have electric hook-ups only.

Your Volunteer Services will support the work of the National Park Service to preserve and protect our natural, cultural, and historical resources so that all may experience our heritage.

HOUSING & AMENITIES: Trailer/RV Pads

Description: Must provide own RV/Motorhome.

****

Interpretation

Description: Assists the Interpretation branch of Big Cypress by acting as a uniformed representative of the National Park Service, displaying professionalism when on and off duty, inclusive of living on a government trailer pad site.

*Must enjoy interacting with the public and the Big Cypress staff.

*Must display enthusiasm and knowledge of wildlife, wildflowers, habitats, and ecosystems.

*Must be a team player and display flexibility.

*Must adhere to all safety regulations inclusive of driving government vehicles.

*Must be able to open and close the Visitor Center and the Welcome Center adhering to standard operating procedures.

*Must be able to accurately open and close the Florida National Parks Association registers, doing required computer work and paperwork correctly.

*Must be able to research, prepare and present three different (15 minute) interpretive talks and one hour long boardwalk stroll.

*Must be able to informally rove on boardwalks and scenic drives answering questions, assisting visitors make connections to the resource, and know how to handle visitors breaking regulations, refraining from being confrontational.

*Will assist in the native plant garden at Oasis two hours/week.

*If possible, will assist as the sweep on one of the six canoeing trips offered every two weeks.

*Must have a professional demeanor and have empathy with the visiting public.

Hours: If a single individual, must volunteer 32 hours/week. If a couple, each individual must volunteer 24 hours/week for a total of 48 hours/week.

Uniform: Each volunteer will be issued three shirts, one hat and one jacket. The volunteer must supply khaki or dark brown long pants, socks, and comfortable closed-toed shoes.

RV/Motorhome: Must bring your own.

Your services will support the work of the National Park Service to preserve and protect our natural, cultural, and historical resources so that all may experience out heritage.

HOUSING & AMENITIES: Trailer/RV Pads

****

Campground Host

DUTIES: Campground hosts provide information to visitors on things to see and do at Big Cypress and surrounding areas; assist in registering campers, and help visitors locate campsites. Hosts may perform minor restroom and campground maintenance duties, gather occupancy information, perform fee compliance duties, and keep the campground staff informed of any issues in the campground. If the host observes what is or may be an illegal activity, the host will share that information with campground and/or law enforcement staff. Other duties may be assigned as mutually agreed upon.

WORK LOCATION: Host positions may be assigned between eight campgrounds within the national preserve. Summers can be hot and humid and electrical storms are common. Power outages may occur frequently. A variety of animals and insects such as skunks, gnats, deer, bear, and rattlesnakes are native. The closest grocery or drug stores are located approximately 20 miles away from the preserve. Cell phone service can be unreliable.

SCHEDULE & TIME COMMITMENT: In exchange for an RV site, hosts will work a minimum of 32 hours per week, which includes weekends and holidays. Hosts will have two consecutive weekdays off. Shifts will vary depending upon operational needs.

We are seeking volunteers with excellent customer service skills who like to meet and communicate with a variety of people. A good attitude, the ability to listen, and the ability to relay information are important to this position. A valid driver's license and background investigation is required. As part of their tour of duty, volunteers will be provided with a camping site which includes water, electric, and sewer hookups. Volunteers will need to provide their own recreation vehicle.

Volunteer uniforms (hats, shirts, and nametags) are required and will be issued by the Preserve. A government vehicle may be available. Training, including portable radio operations, will be provided. Campground hosts may be the only immediate point of contact in case of an emergency.

AREA: Big Cypress is located in sunny South Florida on Highway 41 just 30 miles east of Naples and seventy miles west of Miami. Temperatures during the winter months are usually in the 80s during the day and 60s to 70s at night. Everglades City is the closest town with a small grocery, convenience stores, gas stations, and restaurants. The fishing is great!

HOUSING & AMENITIES: Trailer/RV Pads

Description: RV site available with sewage, electricity, water

Biscayne National Park

Astrid Rybeck, Management Assistant (D)

Special Park Uses Permit Coordinator

Biscayne National Park

9700 SW 328 St

Homestead, FL 33033

Park Phone: (305) 230-1144

Direct Phone: (786) 335-3639

Fax: (305) 230-1190

astrid_rybeck@nps.gov

http://www.nps.gov/bisc/index.htm

In response to our email inquiry:

Thank you for your interest in Biscayne National Park's volunteer program.

I will answer your questions one at a time:

How Many Campground Host Positions? *We do not have campground hosts because our campsites are located on islands which are accessible only by boat. There are, on occasion, folks who own their own boats who want to serve as VIP (Volunteers In Parks) Harbor Hosts. They live either locally in their own lodging, or on the islands if housing is available and offered.*

How Many Park or Residential Host Positions? *Seasonally (+/- November through April), we open a maximum of four positions, with space for two RVs*

What kinds of duties will each position be doing, in general? *These VIPs are responsible for front line visitor services to include visitor center staffing, tours and programs, and informal and formal roving procedures. There are also opportunities for light administrative work and other tasks based on qualifications, abilities and interests.*

How many hours per week do you require? *32 hours per week.*

Do the volunteer campsites have electric (what kind 20/30/50Amp)/water/sewer on each site? *We do have hookups for electric and waste. I do not know of their capacity specifics.*

Is there a RV Rig Limit on any of volunteer sites? *I'm not sure I know what an RV Rig consists of. At the same time, I'm not aware of any sort of limitations.*

What other amenities do you offer these volunteers? *(free laundry, firewood, discounts, etc.) Volunteers, just like any member of the staff have use of laundry, kitchen, and fitness facilities. Whenever possible make sure that VIPs have opportunities to attend NPS-offered training (classroom, online and cross-park), outreach, and in-park opportunities that benefit and develop their personal/professional interests.*

Are there any times of the year harder than others to get volunteers and if so, when? *It is more difficult to recruit volunteers in the summer months, which is our slow season. +/- May - October. We do not offer the RV sites during those months due to the oppressive heat, biting insects and the great possibility of evacuations for severe tropical weather events.*

I hope this information is helpful. Please let us know if you have any additional questions.

Respectfully,

Astrid Rybeck, Management Assistant (D)

Special Park Uses Permit Coordinator

Biscayne National Park

Dry Tortugas National Park

John Nicholas Fuechsel, Park Ranger - Interpretation/Volunteer Coordinator

Dry Tortugas National Park

P.O. Box 6208

Key West, FL 33041

(305) 224-4210

John_Fuechsel@nps.gov

http://www.nps.gov/drto/index.htm

Hello Jolene,

My name is Nick Fuechsel and I am the volunteer coordinator for Dry Tortugas National Park. I would be happy to answer your questions, and if you have any more follow up questions please feel free to respond directly to me.

1. Dry Tortugas National Park is located 70 miles west of Key West FL. There is no option for RVers to bring their RV to the park. Non-RVers can live on island if they pass our screen-out. Due to the logistical complications of living and working on a remote island we need to make sure we get a good fit in one of our volunteer positions before we offer it to anymore. We ask for couples to stay on island for 1 month at a time, which requires them to bring 1 months' worth of food out to the island. We also look for good recommendations, and people with reverse osmosis and photo-voltaic system experience. The volunteer couple is provided with a private bedroom in a shared house on Loggerhead Key. There is A/C, kitchen, bath, and water.

2. We do not have any free extras to offer the volunteers, except sunsets.

3. Other Amenities: None

4. 24/day on call for a month, but generally only a few hours a day of work needing to be done.

5. 1 month min and max.

6. Helping with Cuban Migrant landings, maintaining the electrical and water systems, grounds maintenance, and the occasion visitor interaction.

7. Peak summer is difficult, July, August, and September.

8. Contact me, John Nicholas Fuechsel, John_Fuechsel@nps.gov, 305-224-4210.

Thanks again Jolene,

Nick~

John Fuechsel

Park Ranger - Interpretation

Dry Tortugas National Park

For those of us who do not know or may not be sure what reverse osmosis or photo-voltaic system is, I had to look them up on the internet: Reverse Osmosis is a water filtration system to remove salt from salt water and Photo-Voltaic Systems are solar power systems.

Everglades National Park

Ryan Meyer, Volunteer Coordinator

Everglades National Park

36000 Southwest 8th St

Miami, FL 33194

(305) 242-7015

ryan_meyer@nps.gov

http://www.nps.gov/ever/index.htm

Examples of Positions in the Everglades National Park

Campground Host

Description: Campground Hosts serves the park by greeting visitors and campers and assisting maintenance in the upkeep of this important visitor area.

Duties include:

*Provide information and assistance on a nearly continuous basis to visitors.

*Maintain a residence at the entrance to the campground from approximately Nov 2014 - April 2015.

*Minimum working hours 3 hours per day, 5 days per week.

*Assist campground rangers with camper registration by performing site occupancy checks.

*Observe park visitors and advise those violating park regulations but take no law enforcement action.

*Contact patrol rangers immediately when becoming aware of serious violations or medical problems.

*Advise the Communication Center (Dispatch) of campground events when no ranger is available/present.

*Assist the campground maintenance person with the stocking of restroom supplies (i.e., toilet paper, soap etc.)

*Assist Maintenance staff in emergency repairs to restrooms such as plumbing, replacement of light bulbs and fluorescent bulbs, unplug toilets, stop overflowing of urinals etc.

*Maintain radio and telephone communications with the park dispatch and patrol rangers on campground activities, etc.

*Assist Interpretation Division with maintenance of bulletin boards, posting programs information, advising visitors of daily and evening activities, etc

*Assist dispatch in locating campers wanted by family or for other emergency reasons.

*Cleaning of campsites such as weeding, painting, picking up garbage left at campsites, cleaning fire rings as needed for efficiency and sanitation purposes.

*Other duties as required by campground supervisor.

Safety Concerns:

Biting Insects; Poisonous Snakes; Toxic Plants; Use of tools; Driving Golf Cart, bicycle riding.

HOUSING & AMENITIES: Trailer/RV Pads

Description: RV pad with full hookups provided

****

Recycle Center Managers, Maintenance staff

Description: Volunteer(s) will assist Everglades National Park's Maintenance Team through various projects including managing the Recycling Center.

Position Duties include:

*Collecting bags of aluminum cans and plastic/glass bottles from recycle containers at various park locations. Load bags into truck and reline recycle containers. Empty paper bins from offices;

*Performing manual tasks involving the collecting, sorting, and moving of large quantities of materials which are consolidated for pickup. Volunteer will assist with operation of a flat-bed truck lift, and will drive government vehicles as assigned. Volunteer is responsible for obeying all safety and health rules to prevent injury.

*Tracking and monitoring recyclable materials on spreadsheet and forms, and provide updates as needed.

Other Duties Include:

Assist the maintenance division in the upkeep of Park resources including; facilities, grounds, and roads. You will be assisting full time employees with painting, plumbing, electrical work, carpentry, cleaning, mowing and weed control.

Knowledge, Skills & Abilities Required

*Knowledge of recycling requirements to collect, sort, and transport to a major collection site.

*Attention to detail and commitment to accuracy for dealing with numbers and specifications.

*Ability to interpret oral & written instructions and complete tasks by following a sequence of directions.

*Ability to safely operate light vehicles and equipment. Valid state driver's license required.

*Knowledge of safe methods of lifting and moving heavy items in order to prevent personal injury or injury to coworkers, or damage to trash trucks and/or other containers being moved.

*Must be capable of working for short periods of time on tasks requiring heavy exertion. Very heavy physical effort needed in performing such tasks as frequently lifting and moving objects weighing up to 50 lbs. The work requires frequent bending, reaching, lifting, and walking.

HOUSING & AMENITIES: Trailer/RV Pads

Description: A full hook up RV site with a 50 AMP electrical service.

****

EVER, Interpretive Seasonal Volunteer(s)

Description of Work Duties:

Everglades NP is a busy and complex work park. Primary duties include visitor services such as staffing the Visitor Center, delivering high quality interpretive programs up to two hours in length, some moderately strenuous and assisting with special events. The incumbent(s) will be able to work independently after attending the required seasonal training during the first two weeks of December. Busy 8 hour days begin as early as 7AM and end as late as 5:30PM and incorporate driving a government vehicle, interacting with visitors from around the world while providing directions, information or interpretation as appropriate. Other duties may include trail trimming, trash collection, light cleaning including use of vacuum, dusting, wiping counters and limited sweeping and mopping. Further incumbent may assist at the Reception Desk answering phones and greeting visitors coming into the Headquarters building.

Goals/Outcomes of Job:

To make safety a primary focus before all else. To increase the understanding of park resources to promote appropriate enjoyment and protection of those resources. To maintain facilities in clean and working order.

Benefits to Volunteer:

Learn the integral operations of the Interpretation Division, become intimately familiar with park resources, join a friendly team of staff and volunteers, gain experience in a complex program, and make a positive difference in the experience of park visitors.

Knowledge/Skills/Experience Desired:

Ability to communicate effectively, work an eight hour day, wear the VIP uniform (shirt and hat provided), Flexibility!, able to work as part of team and work independently. Incumbent must be comfortable using computers and familiar with Microsoft Office products, email and use of the internet for research. Further incumbent must drive multiple government vehicles including hybrids. Experience with principles of interpretation a plus but not required.

Work/Sites Location Description: 3 Sites are Available!

*Park Headquarters, located approximately 15-20 minute drive from the two nearest towns of Florida City and Homestead.

*Flamingo District, 38 miles beyond the park entrance, one hour from the nearest town.

*Gulf Coast District, Everglades City, FL. 25 miles south of Naples, FL

HOUSING & AMENITIES: Trailer/RV Pads

Description: Housing: Trailer Pad Provided in Park Housing with Full Hookups - Subject to Grant Funding

Gulf Islands National Seashore

Roxanne Sellers, Volunteer Coordinator

Gulf Islands National Seashore

1801 Gulf Breeze Parkway

Gulf Breeze, FL 32563

(850) 934-2600

roxanne_sellers@nps.gov

http://www.nps.gov/guis/florida.htm

Fort Pickens Campground

1400 Fort Pickens Rd

Pensacola Beach, FL 32561

(850) 934-2622

http://www.nps.gov/guis/planyourvisit/campground-openings-in-florida-and-mississippi-districts.htm

In response to our email inquiry about live on-site volunteer positions

Good Afternoon,

How Many Campground Host Positions? *We have four Campground Host Positions, 3 in Florida to 1 in Mississippi.*

What kinds of duties will each position be doing, in general? *There are 2 Site Host positions, one in Perdido Key and one in Okaloosa, helping maintenance in cleaning restrooms and beach. One furnished apt. Site Host position at the Santa Rosa Area.*

How Many Park or Residential Host Positions? *3 to 4 Historic Structure VIP's*

Do the volunteer campsites have electric (what kind 20/30/50Amp)/water/sewer on each site? *20/30/and 50 amp water/sewer) Camp host and site host have sewer and some Historic Structure volunteers)*

What kinds of duties will each position be doing, in general? *We do have some volunteers that help in the park with other duties depending on division projects, but do not have sewer.*

What is your length of stay limits? *Park asks for a 3 month commitment but can volunteer for 6 months, just not in same position.*

What other amenities do you offer these volunteers? (free laundry, firewood, discounts, etc.) *Laundry facility is offered in some areas. No discounts, firewood, etc.*

Are there any times of the year harder than others to get volunteers and if so, when? *Summer is hotter and of course harder because of heat.*

Campground host positions are on a waiting list because it is full at the time. But we do get cancellations.

Thank you for your interest in Gulf Islands National Seashore.

Roxanne Sellers

Gulf Islands National Seashore

We also found the listing for the Santa Rosa Host position that has a 1 bedroom apartment.

Santa Rosa Site Host

Gulf Islands National Seashore

VIP Job Description – Santa Rosa Area – Maintenance/Fee Operation March 2014

Location and Access:

The Santa Rosa Area (Opal Beach) is located on Santa Rosa Island approximately 5 miles east of Pensacola Beach.

Description of Work:

Opening and closing park gates and restrooms as directed by the District Facility Manager. Picking up trash along roadway shoulders, around picnic shelters and along beaches. Cleaning restrooms that are open(including A and E restrooms when reserved). This includes, but is not limited to, restocking of paper towels, toilet paper dispensers, sweeping and mopping floors, disinfecting toilets and urinals, cleaning sinks and counter tops. Supplies provided by Maintenance. Conduct compliance checks one to two times daily (mid-morning and mid-afternoon) by checking all parked vehicles for display of NPS passes on the dash of visitor's vehicle (Brown envelope stub, GUIS Annual pass or NPS Senior or Access pass). Place a notice to pay fee flyer on the visitor's vehicle (under the driver's side windshield wiper blade) for vehicles that do not have a NPS pass displayed on their dash. Volunteers will not proactively contact visitors regarding payment of fees. Replenish the envelopes for the two iron rangers (Entrance Station on south side and parking lot 6 on north side). After hours public liaison dealing with visitor inquiries, vehicle breakdowns, stuck vehicles, emergencies. Contact dispatcher (934-4050). DO NOT USE GOV'T VEHICLES OR EQUIPMENT TO EXTRICATE STUCK VEHICLES. --- Report any safety concerns or maintenance problems to the District Facility Manger or Maintenance staff.

Working Conditions:

Work is performed outdoors and indoors in all types of weather.

Equipment Provided by the Seashore:

All necessary equipment and tools, including uniform items will be provided. Khaki slacks or shorts may be worn. Blue jeans are also acceptable. Wearing any part of the official NPS uniform or any clothing that closely resembles the NPS uniform is prohibited. The VIP bedroom unit is located on the second floor of the Maintenance/ Ranger Station building at Opal Beach. Bedroom unit is fully furnished and stocked with kitchen dishes, utensils, pots and pans, refrigerator, stove, and bedding. A washer, dryer are located in the maintenance garage for your use and convenience. There is no designated extra vehicle parking area other than where employees park. A Personal vehicle can be parked in the maintenance building bay or under the roof overhang. Recreational Vehicles (RV's) are not allowed to be parked at the Opal Beach VIP site (Parking Space may be available at the Naval Live Oaks Maintenance Compound in Gulf Breeze).

Knowledge and Skills Required:

Must have a cheerful disposition and be able to work with others and the general public. Must have the ability to work under minimal supervision. Must have a valid driver's license. Skills in the safe use of basic hand tools and small power tools are helpful, but not essential. Basic knowledge of carpentry and plumbing is also helpful, but not essential.

Training:

Instructions will be provided verbally, or written, by the Park volunteer coordinator or the District Facility Manager. This will include safety training and training in the use of government vehicles.

Time Commitment:

Santa Rosa volunteers are required to work 32 hours a week in addition to providing night and weekend monitoring of the area. They must work a minimum of 3 months. Extensions will be considered on a case-by-case basis.

Supervision:

The Park volunteer coordinator and the District Facility Manager provide general supervision. VIP's are bound by the rules and regulations that govern employee actions.

HOUSING & AMENITIES: Other

Description: Furnished one bedroom apartment. No pets allowed.

Yes, I know this doesn't really pertain to us Full-Time RVers but I thought it deserved a mention anyway. If you have some kind of monies coming in to pay for your food and are a "handy" type of person this is a pretty sweet deal. Especially for a writer, photographer or some other type of artist who needs some place that may inspire you. Once you close the gates at night it sounds like you will pretty much have the place to yourself. You just never know what you can find available out there.

****

Here is the Historical Position Information that Ms. Sellers mentioned in her email:

Historic Preservation

Description: This program is designed to give volunteers an opportunity to work on historic structures. The duties include Vegetation Control (forts, batteries, buildings, cannon exhibits, trails, seawall and cemetery); Painting (prep, prime and paint metal doors and stairs, wood doors, siding and ramps, cannons, concrete, drawbridges and crank systems, exterior windows, Water Battery walls, batteries & their interior rooms); Masonry (repointing and re-laying bricks on forts, repair concrete on batteries, repair brick paver flooring, water proof building chimneys); Carpentry (replicate screen doors and window screens, replicate fort doors, replicate historic building windows, repair historic buildings, drawbridges and ramps, install privacy fences and boardwalk handrails); pressure wash concrete batteries and fort and Water Battery scarp walls; install and document crack monitors on forts.

HOUSING & AMENITIES: Trailer/RV Pads

Description: RV site available with sewage, electricity, water

WOW, this sounds like a whole lot of work and a project that is going to last a while. But if you are into restoring historical buildings then this just be a good deal for you. Plus, you get a FREE campsite on the Gulf of Mexico!

Timucuan Ecological & Historic Preserve

Emily Palmer, Volunteer Coordinator

Kingsley Plantation- Timucuan Preserve

11676 Palmetto Ave.

Jacksonville, FL 32226

(904) 251-3537

emily_palmer@nps.gov

http://www.nps.gov/foca/index.htm

The Timucuan Preserve includes **Fort Caroline** and Kingsley Plantation.

Fort Caroline National Monument

12713 Fort Caroline Rd.

Jacksonville, FL 32225

(904) 221-5568

Kingsley Plantation

11676 Palmetto Ave

Jacksonville, FL 32226

(904) 251-3537

In response to our email inquiry for live on-site volunteer positions:

I would be more than happy to answer your questions.

How Many Campground Host Positions? *We have no campground host positions as we do not have camping at our main sites.*

How Many Park or Residential Host Positions? *We have space for 2 RVs (meaning max 4 VIPs) at Fort Caroline and residential space at Kingsley in the lodge for up to 6 people.*

What kinds of duties will each position be doing, in general? *All positions are visitor services although light gardening in our interpretive garden may be assigned.*

How many hours per week do you require? *32 hours per week*

Do the volunteer campsites have electric (what kind 20/30/50Amp)/water/sewer on each site? *The RV pads have 30 and 50 Amp power, water and sewer.*

Is there a RV Rig Limit on any of volunteer sites? *We can accommodate rather large RVs but Ranger Craig at Fort Caroline knows the specifics call him at (904) 641.7155 for details if you decide that is the spot you would be interested in volunteering at.*

What other amenities do you offer these volunteers? *(free laundry, firewood, discounts, etc.) There are laundry facilities onsite but detergent is not provided.*

Are there any times of the year harder than others to get volunteers and if so, when? *We are booked most winters meaning January-March outside of this our numbers are lower.*

Feel free to give me a call at the number below if you have more questions.

Emily Palmer

Kingsley Plantation- Timucuan Preserve

We talked to a volunteer in the Visitors Center during our last visit to Fort Caroline. She and her husband have been coming back for several years and enjoy the work and the park staff is very helpful and appreciative of the volunteer's service. As to the Kingsley Plantation, we found a recent listing on the http:///www.volunteers.gov website. We have posted it below.

Visitor Center Hosts

Kingsley Plantation

Duties: Volunteers provide essential services to park visitors on a daily basis. Primary duties include greeting and orienting visitors in the Visitor Center, answering questions about the park, recording statistical data, making sales, professionally answering phone calls, and other office functions. Park volunteers may also assist rangers in interpretive and educational programs and developing exhibits or bulletin boards.

Skills: Good oral communication skills and an interest in natural and cultural history. Volunteers should be flexible, people-oriented, and have the ability to interact with visitors of varying age groups and cultures.

HOUSING & AMENITIES: Other

Description: Free housing in riverfront lodge in exchange for 32 hours per week. All rooms are air conditioned. Volunteers receive their own bedroom with private bath;

rooms for couples and singles are available. Communal area includes TV, VCR, stereo, and fully-stocked kitchen. Laundry facilities are available on-site. There are opportunities for kayaking, hiking, biking, and fishing on the island. Complimentary Access Pass to Florida State Parks.

I don't know but this sounds like a pretty sweet deal folks! The Kingsley Plantation is a gorgeous place to visit and if you could live there, well, you have just got to give it a try.

U.S. Army Corp of Engineers

Lake Okeechobee Waterway

Phillip L. Hart

1660 S. Franklin Lock

Alva, FL 33920

(239) 694-2582

phillip.l.hart@usace.army.mil

Lake Okeechobee - Recreation Area

*Ortona South-Lake Okeechobee - Campground

*St. Lucie South-Lake Okeechobee - Campground

* W.P. Franklin N - Lake Okeechobee – Campground

Positions in the Lake Okeechobee Waterway area are highly coveted and hard to get. They are very rarely advertised on the Volunteer.Gov website. We have emailed the volunteer coordinator and left a message to try and get more information but haven't received a response to any of our inquiries. The only response we received from our email is the name and email address of the coordinators. We haven't tried calling the 800 number but if you are interested in trying to get a volunteer position with the U.S. Army Corp of Engineer's campground give them a call. And you can go online at their website: http://www.usace.army.mil/Missions/CivilWorks/Recreation/VolunteerClearinghouse/VolunteerOpportunities.aspx

Example of volunteer position with Lake Okeechobee Waterway:

Lake Okeechobee & Okeechobee Waterway-Trail Maintenance

W.P. Franklin Visitor Center

1660 South Franklin Lock Rd

Alva, FL 33920

(800) 865-8337

volunteer.clearinghouse@usace.army.mil

Suitability: Adults, Seniors

Difficulty: Average

Description: Trail Maintenance: This Position is Year-Round.

Volunteers complete maintenance concerns around the project by weeding flower beds, planting trees, installing wildlife boxes, and general maintenance. Volunteers also maintain established trail shelters located around Lake Okeechobee by mowing, trimming, cleaning fire rings, picking up litter, and general maintenance of the shelters. (Updated 01/02/2014)

HOUSING & AMENITIES: Trailer/RV Pads

Description: Volunteers will be provided a campsite with water and electric hook-ups, access to dump station, shower and laundry facilities within Ortona South Campground.

****

Lake Seminole/Woodruff

Kelly A. Bunting

PO Box 96

Chattahoochee, FL 32324-0096

(229) 662-2001

kelly.a.bunting@usace.army.mil

http://www.sam.usace.army.mil/Missions/CivilWorks/Recreation/LakeSeminole/Camping.aspx

Lake Seminole - Recreation Area (Mostly in GA only about 15% in FL)

We didn't receive a response to our email inquiry to the volunteer coordinator and there has not been any advertising on the Volunteer.Gov website for this area under Florida or Georgia. If you have volunteered here let us know via email: our-great-adventure@whatthehellblog.com

U.S. Fish and Wildlife

Sallie Gentry, Southeast Region Volunteer Coordinator

1875 Century Blvd., Suite 420

Atlanta, Georgia 30345

Phone (404) 679-7293

Fax (404) 679-7256

sallie_gentry@fws.gov

Website to check for the current listings of Live On-Site Volunteer Opportunities with the U.S. Fish and Wildlife Department that is divided into the states where they Wildlife Refuges and Conservation areas located:

http://www.fws.gov/volunteers/VolResidentOpp.html

The website above is pretty great but you really need to contact the National Wildlife Refuge directly for further information about their programs, how to apply and if and when they will have any availability in the future.

They have a very nice spreadsheet on their website about the various NWF with live on-site volunteer positions but it hasn't been updated in over a year and some of the information given is not complete. So, we emailed each of the various NWFs in Florida for more information and to create our own spreadsheet. Below is a listing of the NWFs which responded to our emails and our phone calls.

We are only listing those refuge's that have volunteer RV sites even though Florida has quite a few more. The others are generally only accessible by boat, too small to have volunteers living on site or not opened to the public. We did list one refuge, Hobe Sound, which stated that they are hoping to add some in the future.

Arthur R. Marshall Loxahatchee NWR

Xavier Cathey, Wildlife Operations Specialist

10216 Lee Rd

Boynton Beach, FL 33437

Xavier_Cathey@fws.gov

Cell: (561) 523-6438

Office: (561) 732-3684 EXT. 6011

Fax: (561) 369-7190

loxahatchee@fws.gov

http://www.fws.gov/refuges/profiles/index.cfm?id=41560

https://loxahatcheefriends.com/

Below are the answers to the questions you have requested. Please let me know if I can be of any more help to you. Thank you and have a great day.

How many Live On-Site Volunteer Positions are there for your refuge? *3 RV pads*

If campsites provided do they include Water/Electric/Sewer and if no sewer is there a dump station nearby? *Yes, Water/Electric/Sewer*

Please specify the electrical types of amps provided (20/30/50) in the electric boxes. *30/50amps*

Is there a RV/Trailer Rig Length Limit on the sites? *50 feet max*

What, if any, FREE Extras (such as Washer/Dryer/Extra Shower/extra storage/extra refrigerator/freezer) do you give to the volunteers? *Washer and Dryer*

What other amenities, if any, do you provide to your volunteers? (a stipend, propane allowance, local phone service, cable, etc.) *Propane*

Where are the volunteer sites/accommodations located (within the refuge or somewhere else)? *On refuge beside our bunkhouse that the interns use*

What is the average amount of hours required per week? *25*

What is your length of stay limits (Minimum and Maximum)? *No limit*

Please list examples of the duties required of the volunteers? *Carpentry, Refuge upkeep, painting, plumbing, mowing, pressure washing, trash, tours, nature walks, visitor center, public use, etc.*

Are there time(s) of the year when it is harder to get volunteers and if so when? *Summer is the hardest time of the year to have resident volunteers because of the weather*

Who would we contact to volunteer at your refuge? (name, phone number and email address) *Xavier Cathey, (561) 735-6011, Xavier_Cathey@fws.gov*

****

Crocodile Lake National Wildlife Refuge

Jeremy Dixon, Refuge Manager

P.O. Box 370

Key Largo, FL 33037

(305) 451-4223

(305) 872-0774

jeremy_dixon@fws.gov

crocodilelake@fws.gov

http://www/fws.gov/nationalkeydeer/crocodilelake/

1-Volunteer Position with a back-in type RV space, tow vehicle parking, a deck, full electrical (30/50Amp) and water hook-ups, solar powered deck light, and limited sewer hook-up. A shared shower and laundry facility is adjacent to the camp area. 24 Hours per week per person for couples; 32 hours per week for singles

1 to 4 month Length of Stay

Refuge is closed to the Public but has a Visitor Center and needs volunteers to help man the center, give interpretation talks, cleaning center, etc. They are under the Key Deer National Wildlife Refuge Manager.

Position posted on the www.volunteer.gov website:

Natural Resource RV Volunteer(s)

10750 County Road 905

Key Largo, FL 33037

Jeremy Dixon

(305) 451-4223

jeremy_dixon@fws.gov

Crocodile Lake National Wildlife Refuge is home to several endangered and threatened species, some of which only occur on the island of Key Largo. The Refuge is closed to public use but does offer some environmental education opportunities at the Refuge Headquarters.

The Refuge has only one paid USFWS employee and typically staffs interns and researchers. Most of the work revolves around managing threatened and endangered species and their habitats.

We are looking for people that enjoy:

*environmental education and interacting with visitors;

*carpentry and maintenance;

*creating displays for our visitor contact center;

*invasive plant and animal management;

*leading other volunteers in Refuge work days

Each volunteer is required to work 24 hours per week (for couples) or 32 hours per week (for singles). RV volunteers typically work for a period of 1 to 4 months, usually October to April.

****

Crystal River National Wildlife Refuge

Ivan Vicente, Public Use Specialist

1502 S.E. Kings Bay Dr

Crystal River, FL 34429

(352) 563-2088 Ext 213

Ivan_vicente@fws.gov

CrystalRiver@fws.gov

http://www.fws.gov/crystalriver

3 full hook-up trailer pads; site has water, electric (35 amp, 220v hook-up), cement slab and picnic table. Laundry facilities are located on the site off Hwy 19 near Homosassa Springs.

"Volunteers should plan to commit to a specified period of time, no less than 30 days and no more than 120 days, unless approved by the Refuge Manager. Volunteers will work a schedule of four eight-hour days per person for a total of 32 hours per week (per couple)"

We tried contacting Mr. Vincente several times over the last couple of months but he has not responded to our emails or phone calls as of the publishing of our book. If we get a chance to visit them in the future we will update this page.

http://www.fws.gov/crystalriver/volunteer.html

****

Florida Panther National Wildlife Refuge

Ben Nottingham, Refuge Manager

3860 Tollgate Blvd, Suite300

Naples, FL 34114

(239) 353-8442

ben_nottingham@fws.gov

floridapanther@fws.gov

http://www.fws.gov/refuge/florida_panther/

2 full 50 amp RV hook-ups with maximum 35 foot in length; includes water, electric, sewer, picnic table, washer/dryer, bath house. A severe weather retreat (with generator) is located close by. Weekly road-side garbage and recycling service is provided. Private phone line, satellite connection or Internet access is available, but not provided.

20 hours minimum per week for each if volunteer couple; 32 hours for individual volunteer for a minimum of 3 months and a maximum of 4. Most of the work is done during the weekdays with occasional weekend work when there are events planned.

Spoke to Jessica Sutt about volunteering with Florida Panther NWR, she stated that they have difficulty getting volunteers during the fall months when they are needed the most for all the events the refuge has. They are, generally, booked with regular Workampers every year from January to March and do not really have volunteers from April to about the end of August due to the excessive heat and the drop off of regular visitors.

They rarely use the services at http://volunteer.gov and would prefer to be contacted directly via phone or email: jessica_sutt@fws.gov with your resume and references.

****

J.N. 'Ding' Darling National Wildlife Refuge

1 Wildlife Dr

Sanibel, FL 33957

(239) 472-1100

dingdarling@fws.gov

http://www.fws.gov/dingdarling/

I spoke with Mr. Combs on September 30, 2014 about RV Workamping positions within the refuge. He stated that they now have:

6 RV pads, two with covers, Water/Electric/Sewer on site, 50 Amp electric, a laundry room with 3 washers/dryers, and offer cable and WIFI for the volunteers.

Each volunteer is asked to work 3 – 8 hour days and help with the facilities maintenance, assist the rangers with educational programs, etc.

They do advertise on the http://volunteer.gov website and have an application you can download directly from their website: http://www.fws.gov/dingdarling/volunteering.html

The webpage information is out of date but the application should be the most recent. You can also send him your resume with references directly to his email account.

They need volunteers mostly from May to October as the other months are generally filled with regular Workampers. But you can always request assignments during the "peak season" just in case one of their regular volunteers is unable to come.

****

Lake Woodruff National Wildlife Refuge

2045 Mud Lake Rd

Deleon Springs, FL 32103

(386) 985-4673

lakewoodruff@fws.gov

http://www.fws.gov/lakewoodruff/

Individual work camp volunteers are expected to provide a minimum of 24 hours or 3 days of service per week. Couples must provide a combined minimum of 48 hours or 4 days per week in exchange for a fun, interesting volunteer experience along with RV site. Occasionally, you may be asked to volunteer additional hours to help with special projects or events.

Our RV sites are level and rustic. Each site has a back-in RV space, tow vehicle parking, a deck, full electrical and water hook-ups, and limited sewer hook-up. Laundry facilities are available. Campsites are located on the Refuge but no other camping is allowed.

Visit the link below to download an application.

http://www.fws.gov/lakewoodruff/GetInvolved.html

Finally get an email response to our inquiry:

Wright, Chris

chris_wright@fws.gov

Ms. MacFadden,

Sorry it has taken me so long to get back with you. We have been in the process of refuge manager transition. To answer some of your questions.

*We have 3 camper pads

*Summer is generally the hardest time to get volunteers

*Limited sewer means that we have camper hook ups at each pad to a septic tank, therefore you can dump the waste straight to the tank without moving your RV

*Volunteers, depending on the season, help with office clean-up, go to festivals to represent the refuge, work in the office doing interpretation for visitors, help with maintenance, help with school groups, etc.

*Power and water are free. There is no cable and no internet. Not sure what other benefits you are referring to.

*Our couple volunteers are required to work 32 hrs. a week. That is two eight hour days each. For a single work camper, it is 32 hrs. per week.

*We don't have a volunteer coordinator. You can contact me or our acting Refuge Manager @ (386) 985-4673

I hope that this helps you

****

Lower Suwannee National Wildlife Refuge

Pam Darty, Park Ranger

16450 NW 31st Place

Chiefland, FL 32626

(352) 493-0238 Ext: 223

pam_darty@fws.gov

lowersuwannee@fws.gov

http://www.fws.gov/lowersuwannee/

1 RV Concrete pad. Water, electric (possibly both 30 and 50amps), and sewer hook-ups provided; satellite TV reception is available with your own dish, there is a washer and dryer onsite for the volunteer. The site is located in Dixie County

24 to 32 hours per person; minimum stay 30 days; maximum stay 90 days

Duties include picking up trash, cleaning the visitor's center and assisting the park personnel with maintenance to the grounds and facilities.

I spoke with Ms. Darty about her live on site volunteer positions. She states that she prefers to advertise on http://volunteer.gov beginning in the late summer and early fall months for volunteers for the winter season only. Right now there are just not enough visitors during the late spring to early fall months to justify a live on-site volunteer. She is already booked until 2017 but suggests to we keep looking on the website again next summer for any openings she may have.

****

National Key Deer Refuge

Kristie Killam, Refuge Ranger

179 Key Deer Blvd

Big Pine Key, FL 33043

(305) 872-0774

Kristie_killam@fws.gov

keydeer@fws.gov

http://www.fws.gov/nationalkeydeer/

3-RV Workamping positions for maintenance, visitors center and education programs.

Comes with campsite, water/electric/sewer. They are booked through the end of 2015 must contact Ms. Killam next summer to be considered for 2016. Because the refuge is located on Big Pine Key they have to pay for the removal of the sewage in the tanks once a week and there may be limited fresh water and electric.

RV must be self contained.

****

Merritt Island National Wildlife Refuge

Nancy Corona, Refuge Ranger

PO BOX 2683

State Road 402 (5 Miles East of Titusville)

Titusville, FL 32781

(321) 861-0667 Refuge Headquarters

(321) 861-0668 Visitor Center

Nancy_corona@fws.gov

merrittisland@fws.gov

http://www.fws.gov/merrittisland/

2 trailer pads with full hookup; local phone service available but long distance phone service must be purchased by volunteer; laundry facilities available; Pets are allowed but must be under control at ALL times.

One month minimum commitment and at least three, eight hour days for couples and four, eight hour days for individuals; 180 day maximum stay.

24 hours per person per week 20 hours additional for every third or more in your unit. 32 hours per week are required for a single person.

They are generally booked with volunteers from September to April but almost always need volunteers May to the end of August. General jobs include maintenance, cleaning bathrooms, picking up trash, manning the visitor's center and running errands.

To be considered you will need to mail in your resume with references to Nancy Corona above.

****

St. Marks National Wildlife Refuge

David Moody, Volunteer Coordinator

P.O. Box 68

1200 Lighthouse Road

St. Marks, FL 32355

(850) 925-6121

David_moody@fws.gov

saintmarks@fws.gov

http://www.fws.gov/refuge/st_marks/

Resident Volunteer positions usually begin by late September and run through the first of May. Applications are accepted year-round. Volunteers perform work in the same area of operations such as visitor services, environmental education, bookstore assistant and resource management.

3 full hook-up trailer pads; includes access to garbage and laundry facilities

32 hours a week; minimum 30 days up to 4 to 6 months.

May to November the hardest times to get volunteers must contact the refuge directly to express your interest.

****

Hobe Sound National Wildlife Refuge

William G. Miller, Refuge Manager

P.O. Box 645

13640 U.S. Highway 1

Hobe Sound, FL 33475-0645

(772) 546-6141

FAX: (772) 545-7572

William_g_miller@fws.gov

http://www.fws.gov/hobesound/

I spoke to Mr. Miller on September 30, 2014 and he stated that they have hopes of adding live on-site volunteers spots in the future. If you would like to get on a list to be considered in the future and to help get these positions going please contact him via email with a resume or to just to express your interest in volunteering at their facility in the future.

****

Even though the Okefenokee Swamp is located in Georgia the Okefenokee National Wildlife Refuge is located just over the Florida/Georgia line just outside of Folkston, Georgia. Since they were kind enough to answer our email we wanted to include them here.

Okefenokee National Wildlife Refuge

Gracie Gooch, Volunteer Coordinator

2700 Suwannee Canal Rd

Folkston GA 31537

Office: (912) 496-3200

Cell: (912) 276-4767

gracie_gooch@fws.gov

Thank you for inquiring about the Volunteer Program at Okefenokee National Wildlife Refuge.

How many Live On-Site Volunteer Positions are there for your refuge? *Four*

If campsites provided do they include Water/Electric/Sewer and if no sewer is there a dump station nearby? *Yes*

Please specify the electrical type: *30/50Amps provided in the electric boxes.*

Is there a RV/Trailer Rig Length Limit on the sites? *35'*

What, if any, FREE Extras (such as Washer/Dryer/Extra Shower/extra storage/extra refrigerator/freezer) do you give to the volunteers? *Commons area provides washer/dryers/satellite TV/phone for local calls/phone card needed for long distance/kitchen, and WIFI*

What other amenities, if any, do you provide to your volunteers? (a stipend, propane allowance, local phone service, cable, etc.) *See above*

Where are the volunteer sites/accommodations located (within the refuge or somewhere else)? *Within the refuge*

What is the average amount of hours required per week? *24 hours per couple/per week or 32 hours per person/per week*

What is your length of stay limits (Minimum and Maximum)? *3-6 months*

Please list examples of the duties required of the volunteers? *Maintenance (lawn, upland and water trails, recycling, cleaning restrooms, etc.): Visitor Services* *(day-to day operations of running a visitor center, interpretive/environmental education).*

Are there time(s) of the year when it is harder to get volunteers and if so when? *May-August*

Who would we contact to volunteer at your refuge*? (name, phone number and email address) Gracie Gooch, (912) 496-3200, gracie_gooch@fws.gov*

Please feel free to contact me if you have any further questions.

****

END OF BOOK CREDITS AND AUTHOR INFORMATION

Thank you for reading my book. If you enjoyed it, won't you please take a moment to leave me a review at your favorite retailer?

Thanks!

Jolene MacFadden

CREDITS

Again, we would like to thank all the Volunteer Coordinators, Directors and Managers of the following:

Florida State Parks

Florida State Forests

Florida Counties Park and Recreation Departments

Florida County Camping Parks

Florida Wildlife Management

Florida Water Management Districts

National Forests in Florida

National Parks in Florida

U.S. Army Corp of Engineers in Florida

U.S. Fish and Wildlife Department in Florida

Thanks to all of you who took time out of their busy schedules to answer my many questions!

About The Author

After working in the medical office field for over 25 years I decided to retire and hit the road. My mom and I have been traveling in an old Class "A" RV full-time for about 2 years now. Since we had an older RV, our first time being Full-Time RVers, and my mother's mom is still with us we didn't want to travel out of our home state quite yet.

Initially, we just visited various Florida State Parks, took lots of pictures and then I would write a review of the park and make a video that I uploaded to YouTube. Eventually, we ran out of money and had to figure out how we could still travel. We are making handcrafted items that we offer for sale on our Etsy.com store - http://www.etsy.com/shop/SouthernWomenCrafts, HandmadeArtists.com - https://handmadeartists.com/shop/jolenemacinjax, SquareUp Marketplace - https://squareup.com/market/southern-women-crafts, as well as on my own website: http://jolenesbooksandmore.com. Occasionally, we will do a vendors booth at music festivals and other special events. But, sadly, these are not making us enough extra money…..yet.

After doing some research on the web we learned that a great way to save on campsite fees was to volunteer as campground hosts. We are enjoying helping out when and where we can. This has been a great learning experience as well as a great way to give back to all the state parks we have enjoyed. These adventures have inspired me to write this book about how other people could enjoy this lifestyle too. We, also, hope that this book will inspire more women to get out there to camp and volunteer in our county, state and national parks. Of course, we hope they will write about their own adventures.

This book is also available in eBook format on Amazon and other fine online retailers

Connect With Me

Follow me on Twitter: http://twitter.com/WomenCampingToo

Like me on Facebook: http://facebook.com/SouthernLadiesTravels

Subscribe to my blog: http://our-great-adventure.whatthehellblog.com